The Music of Wild Birds

The Music of Wild Birds

ILLUSTRATED AND ADAPTED BY

Judy Pelikan

FROM

Field Book of Wild Birds and Their Music

BY

F. Schuyler Mathews

ALGONQUIN BOOKS OF CHAPEL HILL 2004

Editor's Note

We're pleased to bring F. Schuyler Mathews's observations on birds to a contemporary audience.

In reading the text, one might notice that most of the woodland singers Mr. Mathews references are male. Rather than presuppose that Mr. Mathews held any prejudice against female birds, one should bear in mind that males in the wild sing more frequently than their female counterparts.

The two main functions of birdsong are to defend territory and to attract a mate, and in the bird world it is usually the males performing these functions. There are exceptions, of course, but generally speaking, males are the predominant singers.

Published by
ALGONQUIN BOOKS OF CHAPEL HILL
Post Office Box 2225
Chapel Hill, North Carolina 27515-2225

a division of
Workman Publishing
708 Broadway
New York, New York 10003

Library of Congress Cataloging-in-Publication Data
Pelikan, Judy.
The music of wild birds / illustrated and adapted by Judy Pelikan from F. Schuyler
Mathews's Field book of wild birds and their music.
p. cm.
ISBN 1-56512-271-2
1. Birdsongs. 2. Songbirds. I. Mathews, F. Schuyler (Ferdinand Schuyler),
1854–1938. Field book of wild birds and their music. II. Title.
QL698.5.P45 2004
598.8—DC22   2003057888

10 9 8 7 6 5 4 3 2 1
First Edition

Contents

Glossary of Musical Terms

Accel. or **Accelerando.** Faster and faster.

Acciaccatura. A short note which is crushed against the principal note, as it were (i.e., both struck at the same instant), but which is instantly released and the principal key held.

Adagio. Slow.

Ad libitum. At pleasure.

Affettuoso. Tenderly; with feeling.

Agitato. With agitation.

Allegretto. A little quick; not so quick as allegro.

Allegro. Quick; cheerful, joyful.

Andante. The same as Moderato; going at a moderate pace.

Animato. With animation.

Ben. Well, good.

Cadenza. A more or less elaborate flourish of indefinite form, introduced immediately preceding the close of the composition.

Cantabile. In a graceful, singing style.

Chromatic Scale. All the tones, intermediate and diatonic, in successive order.

Con. With; as, *con brio*, with spirit.

Cres. or **Crescendo.** Gradually increasing in strength or power.

Da capo. From the beginning.

Da capo al Fine. From the beginning to the end.

Delicato. Delicately.

Diatonic Scale. The five whole tones and two semitones of any key, in successive order.

Dim. or **Diminuendo.** Gradually diminishing.

Dolce. Sweetly.

Dot. A point placed after a note or rest which adds one half to the rhythmical value of the note or rest.

Dynamics. The force of musical sounds. The degrees range from *pp.*, which is the softest, through *p. m.* and *f.* to *ff.*, which is the loudest.

Finale. The end.

Fine. The end.

Forte. Loud.

Fortissimo. Very loud.

Fuoco. Fire, energy.

Glissando. Playing a rapid passage on the piano by sliding the tips of the fingers along on the keys.

Interval. The difference of pitch between two tones.

Largo. Slow.

Legato. Connected; each tone of a phrase being continued until the next is heard.

Lento. Slow.

Marcato. Marked.

Moderato. Going at a moderate pace.

Phrase. A short tone chain which makes sense, but not complete sense.

Pianissimo. Very soft.

Portamento. A gliding of the voice from one tone to another.

Presto. Quickly.

Rallent. or **Rallentando.** Gradually slower and softer.

Ritard. or **Ritardando.** Slackening the time.

Scherzando. Playfully; sportively.

Sempre. Always.

Sforzando. With emphasis on one particular tone; forced.

Sostenuto. Sustained and smooth.

Staccato. Short and distinct; detached.

Syncopation. The displacement of the usual accent, either by cutting it away from the commonly accented beat, and driving it over to that part of a measure not usually accented, or by prolonging a tone begun in a weak beat past the instant when the usual accent should occur.

Theme. A simple melody on which variations are made.

Tonic. The key tone.

Tremolo. A note made to quiver or shake.

Triad. A chord consisting of three tones—i.e., the tonic with its third and its fifth.

Trill. A rapid alternation of two contiguous tones.

Triplets. Three equal tones performed in the time of one beat.

Vivace. Quickly; sprightly.

A Note from the Artist

Early one morning as I was walking to the beach on Cape Ann, north of Boston, I heard a sampling of bird music. It was made up of eight or so bird songs, continuous, with no punctuation or overlap. It occurred to me that there was a professional troupe of birds in town. I looked up to see the source of this performance. At the top of a tall fir tree was a single bird, a Mockingbird who was being everybody. The street was empty due to the early morning hour, but he played for his pleasure and mine.

It was a beginning for me. The music of a wild bird.

A month later I moved up to northern New Hampshire for the summer. I continued my morning walks and heard some of the same bird songs. This, however, was not a one-man show. This was a chorus, a fluid group of voices that ebbed and flowed as I walked along. I began to recognize soloists who chose to perform in particular places designed

to enhance their individual voices. For example, deep in the woods I heard my first Wood Thrush. The Wood Thrush lives in privacy among ferns and mosses, and its intricate, tender song is delicate perfection.

One day I was walking on the edge of a field. Between two birch trees five wires were strung, the ingrown remains of a barbed-wire fence. Three fledglings had perched for a moment, and they looked like a measure of music complete with notes: G, D, and B.

I began to consider the sounds of these birds as their music. I asked my friend John McIlwaine, a naturalist, if he knew whether there was a book that scored the music of wild birds. There indeed was one in his library: the *Field Book of Wild Birds and Their Music* by F. Schuyler Mathews, published in 1904.

Mr. Mathews lived thirty miles south of Franconia, where I now live. He was a musician, a naturalist, and a gentleman. He grew to know and love birds through their music, as I have. He has become a friend. I like to think that some of the birds he observed and knew so well are the fore-bears of my birds. His lighthearted appreciation of them has been a delight to me. I have learned an enormous amount in our woodland concert hall.

When I brought this idea to Mr. Peter Workman, he had the wisdom and the vision to see the unique quality of the material. He placed me in the gracious care of Elisabeth Scharlatt and Andra Olenik at Algonquin Books of Chapel Hill. It has been an honor to work with them. It is with delight that I offer to you, the reader, the musical fruits of our labors. I wish my pleasure to be yours.

—JUDY PELIKAN

Introduction

Why is the singer recorded in all the books, but never his song? Well, the question is a difficult one to answer without finding fault with someone, so it would be best to make this little volume furnish the response. Here it is, musical pieces taken directly from birds that have sung in the field and on the hillside. Whose are the songs—mine? No, I am only the reporter who has listened attentively for a score of vernal seasons to the little feathered musicians of Nature's great orchestra. This volume is literally a field book filled with the musical sayings of American birds.

The birds with their music are the revelation of a greater world, one with such a boundless horizon as that which we view from the mountain's summit, marveling that it is indeed the same narrow world we live in. It is not possible to listen to the melody of the Song Sparrow in early March without realizing that we are released from the cold clutch of winter and set down in the comfortable lap of spring. What does it matter if the squalling interruptions of the Blue Jay disturb that delightful impression. A discordant note somewhere is a phase of life; not all the singers are divine. In fact, the world of music if it is true to life must record a due proportion of flippant jest, idle chatter, squawking disagreement, ragtime frivolity, mooning transcendentalism, and so on.

But of serene, exultant melody in the music of the birds there is plenty. The plainest evidence of it is in the songs of the Thrushes, and we have the convincing proof that their music is built upon definite, primitive scales—scales which the birds used millions of years before man did. Why each species should have developed and retained an established form of song is not difficult to understand. The habits, associations, and environment of the bird have had much to do with the formation of his music, and education all the rest. By education I mean that gradual schooling of the imitative faculty, which, conscious or not, has resulted in the attainment of musical tones at once pleasing to the ear. This book is not the proper medium in which to set forth evolutionary theories of birdsong, but I must emphatically say that the bird sings first for love of music, and second for love of a lady. I put the lady second, for, if he did not love music first he would not have sung to her, and birds, like the rest of us, are a trifle selfish. What we like most we think others will like as well, hence, in a moment of unselfishness we share the object of our selfishness!

I have taken no liberties with the scores, except to make a doubtful

A or B no longer doubtful. All is a literal transcription, not without certain puzzling phases, of course; for who of us have never been bothered by the rapid performances of expert musicians! Naturally, therefore, some of my records are imperfect; indeed, some singers sang a great deal more than I was able to put down on paper.

I trust, however, that no bird-lover will be disturbed by the remarkable records coming from the more talented songsters when he hears what they have done through the interposition of the pianist. If he should doubt my record I would be pleased to introduce him to my bird (or perhaps some other one just as talented) in the field opposite my house, or on the mountainside behind it in the wilds of New Hampshire.

Whether my scores are useful for the purpose of identifying the birds is another matter—one which I must leave for the reader to decide. It is sufficient for me to point out that I recognized the song of the Veery for the first time in the winter of 1884 upon reading a notation of it in an article on bird music by Simeon Pease Cheney, which appeared in *Century Magazine*. Thirty-one years later, on a certain occasion I requested a Boston musician to go to the piano, run his fingers in a particular way over a progression of minor thirds ascending within the diminished seventh and he would have the equivalent of the song of Swainson's Thrush. He did so and instantly reproduced the notes of the musical record found on page 65. He did not see nor did he need to see the written music, the verbal description was enough.

At the same time, for those who do not read or understand music I have not hesitated to introduce within these pages every possible means aside from music which may help in the identification of birdsong. Therefore, in the same chapter on Swainson's Thrush, there is a suggestive scalloped line which also represents the bird's music. Even if there were but one among a dozen of my considerate readers who could read a musical record, that would discount its ultimate value in no respect.

It should also be borne in mind that for one who has always lived both in town and country in an atmosphere of music, the many allusions to musical parallelism within these pages are believed to be as interesting and useful to others as to himself.

Nature's orchestra consists of not one vast mediocre chorus but rather an endless variety of soloists whose voices, filled with tone-color, redundant in melody, replete with expression, and strong in individuality, make up the orchestra which performs every year the glad spring symphony.

—F. Schuyler Mathews

A Musical Key

There is a general idea among many who are interested in birds that musical notation employed to express a bird's song is nearly worthless. Possibly those who are most skeptical in this regard are the ones who don't read music readily. If so, I shall hope that this Musical Key will help demystify those simpler principles of music necessary to a proper understanding not only of the musical records within this volume but of the character of the songs they represent.

Every bird sings his own song; no two sing exactly alike. A sharp and retentive ear for musical form can recognize those subtle differences of pitch and expression which make each song unique. There are, of course, similarities in the songs of birds of the same species, but the differences, nevertheless, are as distinct. There are immense differences in the individual songs of the Vireos, Finches, Orioles, Tanagers, and Thrushes. For lack of intimate acquaintance with the music of a particular bird we think he sings just like the next one—why! Do all roosters have the same crow? No, any farmer knows better than that. One thing stands as unalterable in the song of a given species—that is its consistent rhythm. The rooster's crow, therefore, will ever be thus:

———   — —   — —

Syllables alone cannot express the song of a bird; they are wholly inadequate, if not extremely unscientific. A syllable may be spoken or sung in any tone of voice, therefore it is useless in locating a tone. Such consonants as Q, S, and Z are of use only in defining a particular quality of tone. Now, as bird songs are composed of a certain number of related tones and a limited range of pitch, there is but one way to record them: they must be upon the musical staff!

Oftentimes syllables are very useful in expressing rhythm or time. For instance, one of the best syllabic examples of rhythm is the *Old Sam Peabody, Peabody, Peabody*, attributed to the White-throated Sparrow. Naturally, one would pronounce the name *Pea-bo-dy* evenly; but the bird does not sing this trisyllabic note that way. He sings the first of the three tones to *three* beats, the second to *one* beat, and the third to *two* beats. Only the musical staff can express this accurately.

Success in identifying a bird's song depends more upon the ability to discriminate differences of rhythm than differences of pitch. Every species follows its own unalterable law in rhythmic time.

The most obvious explanation of rhythm is the drum beat. Here it is:

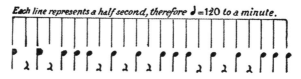

Each line represents a half second, therefore ♩ =120 *to a minute.*

Any child would know what you were representing if you tapped that way on the table. Now the question arises, is there any bird that sings in accordance with a consistent beat? Yes, not only one bird, but forty! Here is the song of the Black-billed Cuckoo:

•• •• •• •• •• •• or this ••• ••• ••• ••• •••

And here is the Robin: ••• ••• ••• • • ••• •••

And the Nashville Warbler: •• •• •• •• •••••

And the Whip-poor-will: • •• • •• • •• • ••

Not one of the little fellows above ever gets his rhythm mixed up with that of the other fellow.

The next step is to become familiar with those mechanical divisions of pitch which the musical staff represents. Pitches in the Western even-tempered scale are separated by regular intervals, although the little bird does not always heed his intervals. He very often sings sharp or flat. (Strictly speaking, no person can sing with a mathematically accurate pitch; we simply come a great deal nearer to the note A than the bird does. So, it is well to remember at the outset that there are some very dubious pitches which come from Nature's orchestra.) The simplest demonstration of well-separated pitches in connection with the rhythm will be found in the song of the Peabody Bird:

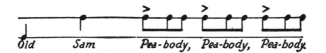

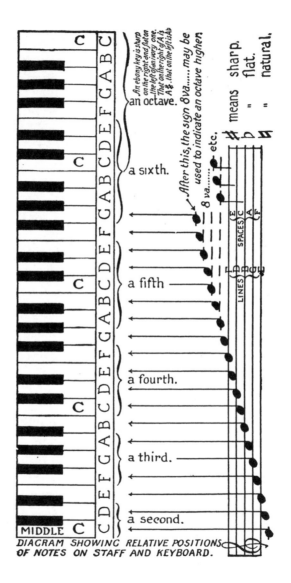

DIAGRAM SHOWING RELATIVE POSITIONS OF NOTES ON STAFF AND KEYBOARD.

The little fellow sings an interval of "a fifth," that is, he sings A, perhaps, and jumps over B, C, and D to E. The musical staff shows this as clearly to one who *cannot* read music as it does to one who can:

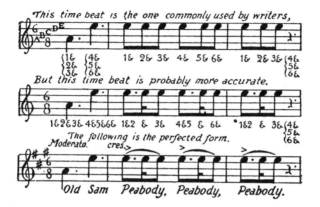

The so-called interval of a *minor third*, common in the Field Sparrow's song, is that which includes only one ebony key between the three ivory ones on a piano keyboard. For instance, D, E, F and E, F, G and A, B, C and B, C, D include only a single ebony in their combinations; all other thirds include two, and are called *major* in contradistinction to *minor* thirds.

The so-called slur, or dash connecting two or more notes, is of utmost importance in expressing their character. The explanatory diagram showing the values of the notes demonstrates also the value of the slur in connection with the syllables *Pea-bod-y* which the Peabody-bird sings. In the case of this slur connecting two notes separated by *an interval*, as in the Eastern Wood-Pewee's song, it indicates that the

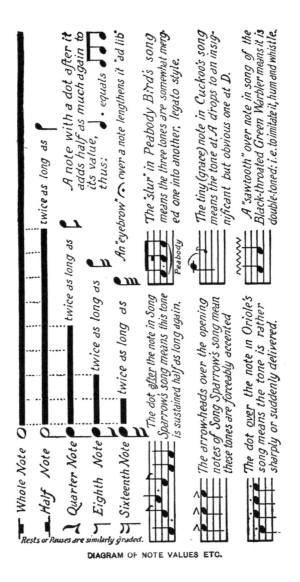

DIAGRAM OF NOTE VALUES ETC.

whistle touches by *even gradations all the intermediate tones*. On the contrary, a simple dot over a note expresses the idea that the tone must be given in a *percussive* manner.

My sawtooth sign is borrowed from the trill sign in music. This sign means to express a *double* tone, which may be demonstrated by whistling the note indicated and humming simultaneously the bass tone at G or G-flat, the second one below middle C, or, for that matter, any deep tone convenient to the whistler. The songs of the Scarlet Tanager and the Yellow-throated Vireo are strongly characterized by this overtone.

Nearly all birds sing in strictly measured time. Some sing one perfect bar, or measure, and others sing several bars. The Whip-poor-will, for instance, sings an endless succession of bars in accurate six-eight time, that is, within each bar (which is marked off on the staff by simple perpendicular lines) will be found six eighth notes or their equivalent in notes or pauses thus:

The time 6/8 is therefore placed alongside of the key signature of *one flat* (which is *B-flat*)—which means the bird sang in six-eight time in the

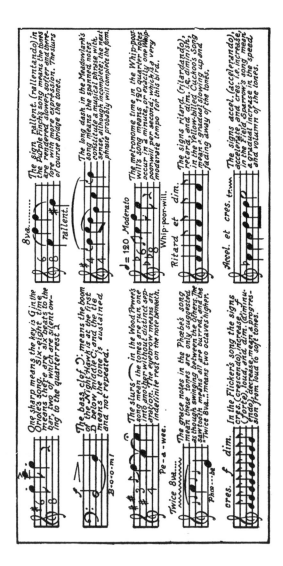

key of F. Again, the Black-billed Cuckoo will frequently sing in two-four time, and we will find two eighth notes and a quarter rest (all of which is the *equivalent* of two quarter notes) in one bar:

The matter of time-keeping is one of the most important elements of music. And although a singing bird does not keep time with any greater degree of accuracy than the artist, pianist, or vocalist, he does keep it with all the accuracy that art demands, and that is more than sufficient for our purpose.

The piano arrangements here are meant solely to demonstrate the musical content of the bird's song. Bird sounds can scarcely be recognized with the assistance of the piano. If one desires a tonal imitation of the song, it must be whistled in accordance with its notation and in exact pitch, no other way will answer.

The question arises as to whether birds' songs are radically different from our own human music—and whether they may be truthfully and logically recorded upon our musical staff. That question is the object of this book to answer affirmatively, and with due regard for all the difficulties involved.

Black-billed Cuckoo

In our American Black-billed Cuckoo, we have a musician who appreciates the value of measured silence. The distinct feature of the Cuckoo's song is the rhythmic recurrence of the rest. No other bird sings exactly this way. This is a thing easily recognized by both musically trained and untrained listeners. I can perfectly demonstrate the principle by a series of dots to represent the notes, thus:

•• •• •• •• •• ••

But the bird does not always stick to couplets,

♦ ♦ ♦   ♦ ♦ ♦   ♦ ♦ ♦

nor does he particularly favor triplets,

♦ ♦ ♦   ♦ ♦ ♦ ♦   ♦ ♦ ♦

Nor is he unmindful of the fact that even in music, variety is the very spice of life:

♦ ♦   ♦ ♦   ♦ ♦ ♦   ♦ ♦   ♦ ♦ ♦   ♦ ♦ ♦

It is apparent, then, that however irregular the number of the notes, the principle of rhythmic pause remains consistent. So perfectly timed is this pause, that upon setting the metronome to the song the bird will be found singing with almost mechanical accuracy.

Cou-coo, cou-coo, cou-cu-coo, cou-coo, cou-cu-coo, cou-cu-coo.

I have long been of the opinion that the Cuckoo's song is set in two distinct tones. Children mark the Cuckoo's well-known song, crying

Cuc-koo.

In the case of the American species it has simply been a question of its ability to separate or individualize those tones. The European Cuckoo does that to perfection, and he has been celebrated most thoroughly by the musician, the poet, and the Swiss manufacturer of clocks.

One of the most beautiful poems in the English language is that by John Logan, *To the Cuckoo*, written somewhere about 1775, and beginning:

> Hail, beauteous stranger of the grove!
>> Thou messenger of Spring!
> Now Heaven repairs thy rural seat,
>> And woods thy welcome ring.

And he does not forget the natural imitativeness of the child, for he continues:

> The schoolboy wand'ring through the wood
>> To pull the primrose gay,
> Starts, the new voice of Spring to hear,
>> And imitates thy lay.

The immortal Beethoven recognizes the perfection of simplicity in the Cuckoo's song, for near the close of the "Scene by the Brook" in the *Pastoral* Symphony he introduces the two familiar notes along with the trill of the Nightingale and the call of the European Quail, thus:

The popularity of the Cuckoo goes as far back as the time of Queen Elizabeth I, and he already appears an acknowledged musician, for Shakespeare writes,

> The finch, the sparrow, and the lark,
> The plain-song cuckoo gray.

The estimate of the great poet is close to the truth, for the song, a drop of the minor third, is one of the commonest occurrences in old-time plainsong versicles and responses, and was actually introduced by John Merbecke into the closing sentences of the Lord's Prayer.

CUCKOO! CHERRY~TREE.

Joseph S. Moorat,
arr. by F.S.M.

(A melody composed of practically but two tones.)

Cuck-oo!

cherry-tree, catch a bird & give it me:—

One of the best things that
has ever been written with the
Cuckoo's song for the theme is
the nursery melody "Cuckoo!
Cherry-tree" by the English
musician Joseph S. Moorat.

Let the tree be high or low, Let it rain, hail or snow. Cuck-oo!

The Yellow-shafted Flicker is a bird of character, otherwise he would never have accumulated so many labels: Wake-up, Yarrup, Piut, High-hole, Woodwall, Yellow-hammer, Yucker, Flicker, Hittock, Clape, and Harry Wicket.

Yellow-shafted Flicker

The Cuckoo knows the value of silence, the Flicker does not. The Flicker is a noisy, aggressive bird, who publishes his whereabouts immediately upon his arrival with a clamor equal to that of the hysterical hen announcing the new-laid egg. The Flicker is a joker in the fullest sense when one catches sight of him bowing and scraping to the other sex in a series of bobs up and down with tail and wings stiffly outspread, uttering the while a significant, *you-see, you-see!* The Cuckoo, on the contrary, is a retiring, quiet character who falteringly and soothingly announces his return to the "old stand" with due apology to those who may possibly disapprove. The Cuckoo runs along rhythmically with his song, thus:

dim.

◆◆　◆◆　◆ ◆◆　◆◆　◆ ◆◆　◆◆

The Flicker keeps straight on with the clattering tongue of a termagant, thus:

cres.

◆ ◆ ◆ ◆ ◆ ◆ ◆ ◆ ◆ ◆ ◆ ◆ ◆ ◆ ◆ ◆

How absolutely different are the characters of the singers, and how perfectly manifest in their songs! The Flicker sounds as if he were whistling for the dogs to drive him off, the Cuckoo sounds as if he were expostulating against such rude treatment. The Flicker's voice resembles a monotonous fortissimo performance on the oboe, the Cuckoo's a pianissimo response from the ocarina.

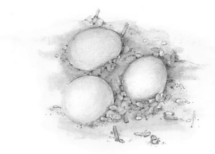

It is not easy to determine the pitch of the Flicker's voice because of its peculiar timbre—it is certainly not a whistle, yet one can easily imitate it by whistling with due regard for the grace note:

But I never could promise that the interval of E to G on the oboe would exactly imitate the voice of the next Flicker that we happen to hear—their voices all differ.

Most writers render the Flicker's song thus: "wet, wet, wet, wet, wet, wet, wet . . ." When he begins to shout his monotonous information about the rain, all other birds may as well remain silent, for his clamor makes the welkin ring!

One never sees the Whip-poor-will perched crosswise on anything. The position is invariably a squatting posture, the legs completely hidden, and the body parallel with any narrow perch, such as a rail or a stick of wood. It is evident the creature would be unable to balance itself the other way.

Whip-poor-will

Mary Johnston in the opening sentences of *To Have and to Hold* makes this rather picturesque allusion to the Whip-poor-will:

> The birds that sing all day have hushed, and the Horned
> Owls, the monster frogs, and that strange and ominous fowl
> (if fowl it be, and not, as some assert, a spirit damned) which
> we English call the Whip-poor-will, are yet silent.

The Whip-poor-will sings during the early hours of the evening, or all night if it is a moonlit one and the springtime. There is something un-canny about the nocturnal bird and his strange song, particularly as he is always heard and seldom seen. By imitating the song I have lured one to such close quarters that the wings have almost brushed my hat.

The song is weird; there is nothing like it in all of Nature's music. It is a perfectly rhythmical, metallic whistle which could be written out intelligibly by a series of dashes, thus:

But these do not carry with them any idea of pitch, and so perfectly does the bird conform to pitch as well as rhythm that one has no difficulty determining the key of any one of the three tones. Here is an example of two distinct intervals of a fourth and an octave—it is perhaps the commonest form of the song:

But no two birds sing exactly alike. Listen and you will hear a distant bird respond in a lower key, with a lesser interval, and in slower time:

Then another individual very near at hand will consider this entirely too slow, and start in vigorously and vivaciously, thus:

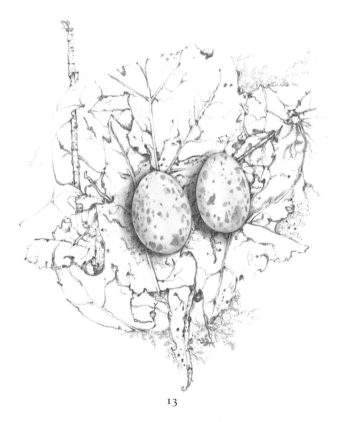

That seems to be altogether too flippant a measure for the next soloist, so he corrects the time and the key according to his own ideas:

Observe that he has confined his song to an interval of only a major second, and is proceeding in a very leisurely manner, when he is interrupted by someone else who attempts a compromise between extremes on an entirely different key:

Apparently this variety in the manner of chastising "poor Will" has exhausted the patience of bird number six, and he breaks in on both the others with an emphatic and vociferous insistence on the original key,

F, but even he must impress his own personality on the song so he proceeds in F-minor:

I confess that I have picked out from my collection of Whip-poor-will annotations these six songs in correlated keys for the purpose of showing the generally harmonious relationship of bird music. It would indeed be a rare occasion if the six occurred in the regular succession given above, but there is every chance in the world that we will hear something very similar to this the next time we listen to a number of Whip-poor-wills singing together. This bird is Nature's virtuoso of the nocturne, and it requires little study to discover that few, if any, of the renderings are exactly similar.

Here is the kettledrum of Nature's orchestra! This talented performer cannot be excelled in his wonderful accelerando.

Ruffed Grouse

W ho?"—to quote William Hamilton Gibson—"Who will show us the drum?" Nearly all of us have seen the Ruffed Grouse, many of us have heard the drumming, but the "drum" of the Ruffed Grouse remains a most mysterious practice of this favorite game bird.

There has been no end of theorizing by eminent naturalists and others interested regarding the way the Ruffed Grouse drums his drum. I think all opinion may be set aside in the face of the fact that the sound is produced by the concussion of air caused by the rapid movement of the wings. The wings appear to strike the breast, but in reality they do not. For close observation shows that the wings are brought considerably forward while the body of the bird is stretched to a position as nearly perpendicular as possible. It is the air that booms under the rapid lashing of the wings, just as it is the air which sings in a baritone voice through the primaries of the Nighthawk's wings as he drops like a shot through the sky.

It is rather difficult to locate the tone of the Ruffed Grouse's kettle-drum with exactness, as it lacks life and character, but it may distinctly be heard at a distance of a quarter of a mile or more. That said, the tone of the Partridge's kettledrum may be safely recorded at A-flat as well as at A, or at B-flat.

The first tones are staccato, and widely separated, but the last are run together in a rapid roll, thus:

Upon seeing the bird go through this remarkable performance one is struck with amazement, for at the end he subsides into utter quiescence instead of flying all to pieces! Why the stump or the rock on which he is perched is not covered with every feather from his body it is difficult to understand. But no, he still holds together, and probably if one waits a few more minutes he will be at it again. Watch him closely, and presently the head begins to bob up exactly like that of a rooster before he begins to crow, now the wings are spread and jerk back and forward with a hollow thud at each movement, and the next moment the whole bird is a blur of feather and the air is filled with a rushing whir which is swiftly graduated to a finish as the body of the creature becomes distinct and quiet once more. Then he drops into the forlornest of attitudes, looking as if he would never move again.

Bobwhite Quail

B_{ob} . . . *white!* As his name implies, the Bobwhite Quail's song simply combines two tones admirably represented by the syllables, *Bob . . . white!* But one must whistle them, or do the difficult trick of whistling and saying the words simultaneously. Nor is this all: the word *bob* should be rendered staccato—it must fairly bounce like a ball, and the *white* should be a long slurred tone extending all the way from *bob* to the end of *white*.

To illustrate the song by the aid of the piano one should strike F (the third one above middle C) quickly, as though the ivory were hot, and again the second time, jumping at once from it up to D-sharp. This is what a musician would call an augmented sixth, and that is what may be considered the nearest approximation to the range of the Quail's voice.

The Quail does not always whistle F or make a jump as high as a sixth. Song no. 4 is what the bird gave me in the middle of May 1900, in the Arnold Arboretum near Boston. The key is the same, but the bird began on E-flat, and jumped from F up to B-flat. It need not be supposed that the Quail confines himself to *bobwhite* either, he frequently throws in an extra *bob,* as you'll see in song no. 3.

There was a children's May-song, popular, I remember, in the public schools of New York years ago, which began with the Bobwhite's call, in a sixth:

Eastern Wood-Pewee

The sighing of the pines is not more expressive of mournful fancies than the sobbing of the little somber-colored Pewee. Among all the singers of the woodland he is the sentimentalist. The Pewee's short song of three or four notes appeals to us wholly by reason of its apparently emotional nature, not unlike the famous old Irish melody, "The Last Rose of Summer." *Pee-a-wee* he sings, and then after an unreasonably long pause, he adds, *peer!*

Whistle with the familiar run down the musical scale, just as though someone stepped on your toe, or you were greatly surprised or shocked. If that is done in the laziest possible manner, the Pewee's *peer* is accurately imitated. It is no presto performance, it must be decidedly largo, and when the lowest tone of the scale is reached it must be sustained for at least a second. Then, for the better part of the bird's song, his *pee-a-*

wee, all that is required is to whistle in a very slow, dragging fashion, first a clear high note, then one exactly a fourth below that, and finally one a minor third above the one last mentioned.

The Eastern Wood-Pewee does not attempt to hit a note squarely, but rather reaches for it with all the sentimentality of the inexperienced and uncultivated singer, capturing us in spite of his error by the perfect sweetness of his voice. Note how dignified and graceful his rendering is of that familiar but rather flippant aria in Auber's *Fra Diavolo:*

The Pewee takes this juggling more seriously, and sings with feeling:

There is an ineffable grace, almost a religious solemnity to the little melody when it is sung that way. Whether at matins or vespers the Pewee's song is always the same, slow, peaceful, restful, and thoroughly musical.

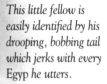

This little fellow is easily identified by his drooping, bobbing tail which jerks with every Egyp he utters.

Least Flycatcher (Chebec)

The Least Flycatcher's call of two short syllables is the origin of his old common name—a perfectly evident, squeaky and rapid, *chebec.* Pronounce the word *Egypt* in a stage whisper as rapidly as possible, but be sure to drop the final *t* and you have the call note.

Four times 8va. or higher than you can go?
presto.

Egyp-   Egyp-   Egyp-

Under the influence of some unusual excitement one hears, *Egyp, Egyp, tremble-emble! Egyp, tremble-emble!* Whether that means a fateful warning of invasion to the ancient country or not, it is difficult to say.

Blue Jay

The advent of a horde of Blue Jays, about the middle of July, in the vicinity of my studio means a general dissipation of all the songbirds for the time being. There is at once a rumpus in the old orchard, and a continual flash of blue wings in the sunlight—many little brown wings, too, take flight to return no more. For the Blue Jay is the rascal of the bird community, the bully and tease of all creatures smaller than himself.

The Blue Jay's call is a squalling cat like

And occasionally a clear, bell-like, very musical three-syllabled phrase is heard:

Again, a perfectly clear whistled but metallic-toned octave strikes the ear, thus:

Despite the confusion and the harsh ringing *jay, jay* tone, there is a decidedly musical element in the Blue Jay's voice. He gives us a perfect octave, and that is a great deal more than the Bluebird can do.

The Blue Jay is a robber. He not infrequently attacks other birds engaged in nest-building, drives them off, and finishes the job to his own liking.

Crow

The Crow has his enemies, plenty of them, and few if any friends. Still, when he is tamed, the Crow is very loyal to his friend and protector, recognizing his voice and answering his call at once.

There is no music in the Crow's *caw*, nor any in the rest of his various calls, but he is a bird with a distinct language: his harsh mutterings are just desultory talk; his *c-r-r-r-r-uck* bespeaks contentment; his sharp and incisive *caw, caw, caw* means "attention!"

Caw! caw! caw!

And his three fortissimo tones, embracing a distinct major third, mean, I do not know what, but I sometimes think, "Come this way quick!"

He takes a conspicuous stand at the top of some dead limb when he sends out this emphatic summons, and it certainly is vehement enough for one to imply that business of a strictly important and urgent nature is pending.

In appearance the male Bobolink and his mate are utterly different, but before the summer is past he changes his costume and dons the sober colors of the female. Not content still, he changes his voice after the nuptial season, and not another liquid, bubbling note do we get from him once he starts in with his monotonous, metallic chink.

Bobolink

The poet William Cullen Bryant's

> Bob-o'-link, bob-o'-link,
> Spink, spank, spink

gives a good representation of the three-syllabled tones in the Bobolink's song, and also a fair imitation of the wiry quality of the tones.

The first part of the Bobolink's song suggests the waltz in tolerably clear whistles set to three-four or nine-eight time. The latter part of the song is a species of musical fireworks. He begins bravely enough with a number of well-sustained tones, but presently he accelerates his time, loses track of his motive, and goes to pieces in a burst of musical scintillations. It is a mad, reckless outbreak of pent-up irrepressible glee. The difficulty in either describing or putting upon paper such music is insurmountable. I have never been able to sort out the tones as they passed at this breakneck speed. But if one prefers not to interpret bird music, but to take it from Nature exactly as it comes, this bit that follows may prove acceptable:

Or this:

I obtained the following annotation of the Bobolink's song at a spot near Smith College in Northampton, Massachusetts:

I have chosen to render the latter part of this song, which is given in rapid, twanging, wiry tones, in a series of comprehensible intervals, not unlike those which Chopin introduced in his fantasias. The bird simply suggested that kind of a "run" to me, that was all. He did not in the least conform to pitch or interval, but the character of the music was the same, and if everybody understands that a fantasia is a musical composition freed from strict form and allowed to follow the lead of fancy, they will see at once that the last part of the Bobolink's song unquestionably conforms to that style.

Cowbird

This disreputable character, parasitic in habit and degenerate in all moral instinct, gets its name through its fondness for bovine society, and its fame from its abominable habit of laying its egg in another bird's nest.

The Cowbird has no song. His nearest approach to music is a sort of guttural murmuring, a harsh, metallic *gluck zee-zee* without rhythm or sentiment. Why should they have either? The bird has no mate to call. He is a polygamist, a bird of no principles, a low-down character. He usually goes with a flock of other evil spirits just like himself, and his favorite resort is the cow-yard or the pasture where the cattle graze.

Very probably Cowbirds have one good, redeeming quality: they keep a myriad of insects in check which otherwise would worry the life out of the cows. But no one seems to be positively sure about that.

Red-winged Blackbird

A beautiful slim and smooth black bird with scarlet epaulets sways unsteadily on the supple stem of a cattail on the margin of the pond, and sends out a strange reedlike note. This is the Red-winged Blackbird, one of the easiest birds to identify by his song.

The song is made up of three syllables, the first of which is obscure and difficult to catch unless one is not very far away from the bird. Various writers interpret the syllables differently. According to Thoreau's way of thinking, it's *conk-a-ree!* Emerson's opinion is that "The Redwing flutes his 'O ka lee' "; William Hamilton Gibson, *gl-oogl-eee;* and yet another writer, *gug-lug-geee.* On two points all seem to agree: the three syllables, and a repetition of the vowel *e* in the last syllable. So, it is an apparently simple matter to express the rhythm by signs, bearing in mind that the doubling up of the vowel *e* must mean a sustained tone. If this is so, then the cabalistic signs should appear thus:

Gug - lug - gee-e-e-e-e-e!

By simply tapping and moving a pencil on a table one can get the rhythm perfectly.

The written music appears almost as plain, although there is never that accuracy of pitch in the Redwing's voice which would enable me to say he uses a perfect third, or fourth, or sixth, as the case may be.

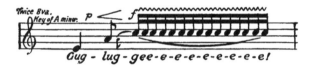

Gug - lug - gee-e-e-e-e-e-e-e!

To be sure, the fellow is pardonably flat at times, and then again distressingly sharp, but on the whole the music is intelligible, welcome, and even inspiring, for it is a joyous announcement that spring is at hand. There is also, as William Hamilton Gibson writes, a felicitous "gurgle and wet ooze in it," which reminds us of the swamp, or the swimming-pool-in-the-springtime coloring which the French artist Corot so much loved to paint.

I call to mind a bulrush-bordered pond in the Middlesex Falls, near Boston, where one lovely spring afternoon I heard a dozen Redwings gurgling away like the rippling of a brook. After studying the singers and their songs for a full half hour, there suddenly dawned upon my mind the unmistakable evidences of concerted harmony in the music. Selecting the songs of six, I arranged them in proper order, then added the words and accompaniment later:

This is really the proper way to study bird music. The responsive character of the song is a strong factor in the complete understanding of it. Half the birdsongs we hear are questions, the other half are the answers.

In spring the male Redwings arrive first, sometimes in large flocks. It is fully two to three weeks later before the rusty-colored females put in an appearance. Then, as might be expected, the conversation waxes lively, and the competitors for mates have a great deal to say about themselves. They "talk" for nearly a month or so before the mating begins.

Brown Thrasher

The Brown Thrasher does not care in the least whether you observe him or not. He holds a conspicuous position from the topmost branches of a tree where he commands an extensive outlook. The business of the song is too important a matter to brook interruption, so he proceeds in an energetic manner with an eye on you and a mental reservation, perhaps, to be on guard lest you approach *too* near.

The Thrasher's music is a medley of rapidly repeated tones not unlike those of the Catbird. But there is an unvarying difference between the songs of the two birds: the Thrasher repeats his notes and the Catbird

does not. Hence, we find that the Thrasher advises the farmer about his
various duties in emphatic insistence, thus:

> Shuck it, shuck it; sow it, sow it;
> Plough it, plough it; hoe it, hoe it!

Watch the graceful little musician as he performs, and note his complete absorption in the music; his long, slender bill is wide open, his
head is thrown back, and his notes are poured forth in rapid succession.
His pauses are rhythmic and almost exactly in accordance with met-

ronome time; his notes are in groups of two, three, four, and even five, nearly every group is repeated once, and each one is in a voice register sharply contrasting with the other. He sings high and he sings low, sometimes with an overpowering overtone, other times with a clear and liquid whistle. Every one of the note-groups resembles some portion of the Catbird's song, yet each is delivered in a manner altogether too loud and emphatic to make one doubt the singer. My notation shows repeated phrases and rhythmic pauses:

Now the Thrasher takes to the top of the big tree with an evident intention to address the whole world—or as much of it as he can see! There he sings his praises exactly as the poet Robert Browning had said:

> That's the wise thrush; he sings each song twice over,
> Lest you should think he never could recapture
> The first fine careless rapture!

*The appearance of the Winter Wren is similar to that of the House Wren:
a fluffy little ball of mottled brown feathers, with a perked-up tail and a bobbing
head all too tiny to belong to a song so loud and ringing.*

Winter Wren

To hear the Winter Wren's song one must journey to the higher mountains where the lively, dancing melody reverberates through the spruce forests like the tinkling of silver bells. This decidedly boreal species is a common resident of the Canadian zone, and breeds from Alberta to Newfoundland, southward to Minnesota, the mountain regions of New York and New England, and along the Alleghenies to North Carolina.

Here is a record of the song taken on the slopes of Mt. Mansfield, Vermont, on July 10, 1908. The high C is the highest on the piano keyboard, and the rapidity with which the song was delivered was almost incredible:

The distinguishing character of this Wren's song is that the initial note of the various trills is accented. I had chanced to be reading Bradford Torrey's *Birds in the Bush*, which says, "The great distinction of the Winter Wren's melody is its marked rhythm and accent, which give it a martial, fifelike character. Note tumbles over note in the true Wren manner, and the strain comes to an end so suddenly that for the first few times you are likely to think that the bird has been interrupted.

It was extremely gratifying to find my bird singing very possibly the same kind of song which Mr. Torrey heard:

The following record was secured in early July 1914, near Lonesome Lake, which lies in the slight depression of the southern buttress of Cannon Mountain in the Franconia Notch. The elevation was about 3600 feet, and the Winter Wrens were singing in every direction among the spruces.

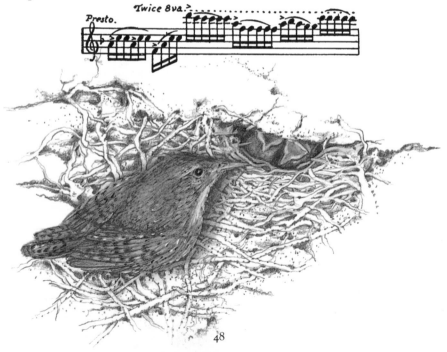

Sedge Wren

This extremely active little Wren is more often heard than seen. He prefers damp meadows and bogs, and you cannot see him without great risk of wet feet and a fight with mosquitoes. It is not easy to obtain even a scraping acquaintance with a secretive little bird who dodges in and out among the grasses and sedges like a frightened mouse!

The snapping call note of this marsh-inhabiting Wren is certainly its most familiar note. It is without discernable pitch and resembles the grating sound of little stones or glass balls striking together.

The same grating note is heard in the monotonous song, though at the height of the nuptial season it acquires something in the nature of a descending trill belonging to a sparrow. The more deliberate opening notes are described as *chap-chap-chap*, but these are absolutely toneless. The rest of the song is erratic but somewhat musical, though I can promise nothing for accuracy in pitch:

House Wren

The House Wren is a tiny bird with an extensive, rippling, laughing song, which reminds one of a musical waterfall or purling brook.

The song's lack of a distinct and full tone is more than atoned for by irrepressible spirit. Beginning sotto voce with an inexplicable jumble of grating sounds, it proceeds with a series of rapid trills from a high to a considerably lower register without pause or slackening of speed. Here are three records taken in Millington, New Jersey; Englewood, New Jersey; and Blair, New Hampshire. There is practically no difference in

the rhythmic form, no great variation in the pitch, and only slight variation in melodic structure:

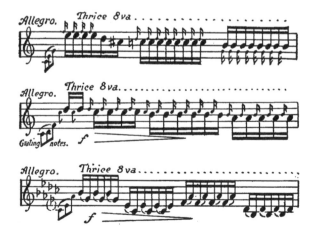

The House Wren's song possesses a rapturous abandon, which at once captures the heart of the listener just as his eyes would be entranced by the sight of a beautiful cascade in a mountain glen. The jubilant music drops like a silvery spray. The songster should have been named Minnehaha—Laughing Water!

Black-capped Chickadee

The entertaining little Chickadee is a favorite among all bird-lovers, and with good reason. Few of our wild birds are so sociable, fearless, and responsive. Whistle to the little fellow and he invariably replies. (One might whistle all day to the Oriole without eliciting the slightest response.) Call the Chickadee in winter, show him that you have something good to eat, and eventually with patience and cautious quietude on your part he will feed from your hand.

This is the bird, too, who braves the winter's cold, and makes himself at home in the dooryards of New England farmhouses, the one of whom Emerson wrote,

> This scrap of valor just for play
> Fronts the north-wind in waistcoat gray,
> As if to shame my weak behavior.

The Chickadee gets his name, of course, from his rather squeaky and harsh call-notes. Every child knows them, *chick-a-dee-dee-dee-dee*, which, however unmelodic, could be placed upon the treble staff thus:

There is no certainty about pitch in such mixed tones as these, but there is an absolute mechanical rhythm. For instance, one must know without a knowledge of music that a person would naturally pronounce the syllables *chick-a* exactly twice as fast as the *dees*. Tap on these dots with a pencil ♦♦ ♦ ♦ ♦ ♦ and you will get the true relative value of the syllables *chick-a-dee-dee-dee-dee*. Lisp the first two notes between your teeth and combine a hum with a lisp for the other four, and you have the Chickadee's call.

The song of the bird is entirely different

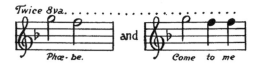

and is often mistakenly attributed to the Phoebe. But the poor tuneless Phoebe is intellectually incapable of such a perfectly musical bit as this. Indeed, few small birds whistle their songs as clearly, and separate the tones by such lucid intervals.

The charm, too, of the Chickadee's singing lies in the fact that he knows the value of a well-sustained half note, another point which should be scored in the little musician's favor. Truly, in this regard he is far ahead of the Canary, for the latter wastes his energy splitting into hemidemisemiquavers every tone within the compass of an octave.

The best way to prove the musical value of the Chickadee's two or three pure tones is to connect together a few such as one may easily obtain from three or four birds which are singing together in their customary, delightful, antiphonal way:

I may be overestimating the value of a melody so meager as that of the Chickadee, but if so it becomes difficult to account for the charm that underlies the music of all great composers, for constructively considered their melodies are mere elaborations of absolutely simple themes.

Veery

The popularly dubbed "skulking Veery" is a shy bird who prefers the thick damp woods beside the river's brink, and the dense undergrowth of low woodlands. He sings a spiral, tremulous silver thread of music far into the evening hours and has, through popular misapprehension, earned the strange title, American Nightingale.

A remarkable and beautiful glissando of overtones, the Veery's song is without clear melody and in a measure without definite pitch. The tone effect at a distance is like the metallic twang of the Jew's harp. The song generally begins with a pianissimo upward run of, perhaps, a minor third, followed by a downward chromatic run repeated once, and finally another downward chromatic run, apparently beginning a minor third or maybe a major third below the other, which is also repeated. The run in both cases is an indefinite one, as it might include a third, a fourth, or even a fifth. The song could be represented in curving lines, thus:

O, veery, veery, veery veery!

Or in musical notation, thus:

Sostenuto. *This and the following records are twice 8va., exact pitch.*

O, veery, veery, veery, veery.

There are variations to this form. For instance, I have often heard a song with four, instead of five, divisions, and with each of the three divisions succeeding the first dropping approximately a third, thus:

I have also heard another variation involving a complete change in the relationship of the tones. In this instance the Veery dropped the chromatic scale and adopted in its stead distinct intervals. This singer was the best of his kind I have ever heard:

The Veery's song is oft considered the most spiritual of all the wildwood singers, for he sings a vesper hymn to the dying day. He so inspires the deepest feelings of the heart at the solemnest hours that Henry Van Dyke penned the following lines in his poem "The Veery."

> The moonbeams over Arno's vale in silver flood were pouring,
> When first I heard the nightingale a long-lost love deploring.
> So passionate, so full of pain, it sounded strange and eerie;
> I longed to hear a simple strain,—the wood-notes of the veery.

Wood Thrush

The Wood Thrush's music steals upon the senses like the opening notes of the great Fifth Symphony of Beethoven: it fills one's heart with the solemn beauty of simple melody rendered by an inimitable voice.

Certainly one of the most gifted of the woodland singers, the Wood Thrush's notes are usually in clusters of three, and these are of equal value. No violin, no piano, no organ confined to such a limited score can appeal to one so strongly.

The commonest one of the clusters is an admirable rendering of the so-called tonic, the third, and the fifth tones, thus:

This is one of the best things the Thrush can do, and he does it splendidly.

There is no doubt about the Wood Thrush's intervals—they compose a perfect minor chord. After a pause of a second or two the bird supplements the minor with the major form a third lower, thus:

Then after that comes something like this, with the last note doubled,

which is immediately succeeded by a pretty relative phrase with a vibrating final note:

Warbling cheerily.

Still the singer continues, and in a burst of feeling rapidly reels off the following:

Tra-la-la-la-z-z-z\

There is a harmonic overtone to nearly all the notes of the song, and frequently a strange and vibrant if not harsh tone succeeds the three-note group, thus:

Undoubtedly the Thrushes possess extremely short and extremely long vocal chords, and probably the latter are vibrated along with the former thus producing a singular effect of harmony. The rapidly repeated resonant note which frequently completes a phrase has a distinct metallic ring which strongly reminds one of the musical ripple of the blacksmith's hammer as it bounces upon the anvil between the blows dealt to the red-hot horseshoe. Could it be possible that the ancestor of this Thrush learned his song near the doorway of Mime's forge?

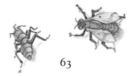

Olive-backed Swainson's Thrush

crescendo.
I love, I love, I love, I love you!

The song of the Olive-backed Thrush is one of the most charming examples of a harmony in suspension in all the realm of music. As the above zigzag line illustrates, the bird deliberately chooses a series of even intervals and climbs up the scale with a thought entirely single to harmonious results. Technically the song is compassed by a diminished seventh; it ascends in two-note groups, the notes evidently separated by minor third intervals with each second note the lower of the two.

Constructively considered, the music strongly resembles these somewhat meandering but soothing phrases in the first movement of Beethoven's *Moonlight* Sonata:

The great composer, however, goes slow and continues the theme. The bird does not, but after giving the third or fourth rapid group of notes, is dissatisfied with the pitch and tries a lower or a higher one, thus:

Like all the northern Thrushes, the Olive-backed is a transcendentalist, who is never satisfied with a creditable effort but must try for something better—and then goes to pieces in the attempt! Here is as near a representation of that idea as it is possible to get; notice how the bird continuously tries for something on a higher key, and finally ends with a jumble of high notes:

66

Hermit Thrush

The song of the Hermit Thrush is the grand climax of all bird music—there is no woodland singer who is his equal. He is a bird of genius; a gentle and retiring spirit; the first of the Thrushes to come, the last to go, the soonest to pipe his joyous lay after the clearing away of the storm, the last to sing the vesper hymn, and the earliest to open the matutinal chorus at break of day.

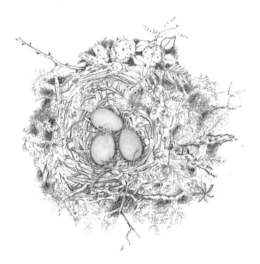

It is necessary to show the nature of this superb songster's preeminence, and that can only be done by comparing his style with that of other birds. According to Daines Barrington's estimate of the comparative merits of English songbirds, the Nightingale scores the highest mark in mellowness of tone and depth of expression. In compass of voice and facility of execution he considers the bird without a rival on the other side of the water. But Barrington did not know the Hermit Thrush, and it is doubtful, if he did, whether British prejudice would allow him to remove the Nightingale from the niche of fame and put in its place an American bird unknown to the poets. The Hermit Thrush is certainly the Nightingale of America. For think what that would mean! Those who have sung the praises of the Nightingale are many and famous: Von Der Vogelweide, Petrarch, Gil Vicente, Shakespeare, Milton, Drummond, Cowper, Coleridge, Byron, Heine, Shelley, Keats, Longfellow, Arnold, Mulock, and Christina G. Rossetti. What a list it is! And shall the Hermit Thrush reach fame through the medium of greater minds than these? I wonder what they would have written in an ode to the American bird. Certainly less about passion and pain, and more about musical bursts of triumph. The passionate and plaintive notes of the Nightingale have no place in the Hermit's song. Our gifted Thrush sings more of the glory of life and less of its tragedy, more of the joy of heaven and less of the passion of earth. That is a purely human point of view all the more significant because one bird sings to the European, and the other to the American ear!

The Hermit Thrush is an altogether different kind of a singer. He is brilliant in execution beyond description, as versatile in melody as a genius, and as pure in his tones as refined silver. The mechanical rhythm is completely overshadowed by the wonderful way in which the singer delivers his sustained tonic and then embroiders it with a rapid and brilliant cadenza. The one prime point which distinguishes the song of this Thrush from all others is the long, loud, liquid-clear tone with which it is begun.

This is completely beyond the ability of the Nightingale. It is a theme worthy of elaboration at the hands of a master musician, but the Hermit does his own elaboration:

Some of the themes are in the minor key and some in the major; some are plaintive, others are joyous, all are melodious. There is no score of the Nightingale which can compare with such records as these.

One of the most fantastic and perhaps extraordinary themes I ever heard from the Hermit Thrush was obtained late in July in the White Mountains:

In structure it closely resembles that tempestuous and wild movement that opens the finale of Beethoven's *Moonlight* Sonata:

But Beethoven emphasizes the tonic at the close of the run. The Hermit does so in the beginning. Both bits of music progress in presto time, and both rush onward to a high climax.

The Thrush, moreover, is a transcendentalist; he climbs higher than his voice will carry, and like many another aspiring songster, makes a ludicrous failure of the highest notes. After one or two bad breaks, which apparently threaten the woodland symphony with the ignominy of disaster, the Hermit—who sings the prima donna's part of the score—seems to say to himself, after a short pause, "See here, my fine fellow, this will never do, that portamento was out of place, and the high note sounded like the whetting of a scythe! Try a lower key and silence that Swainson over yonder mouthing his zigzag notes as though he were trying to make them creep upstairs! Shucks! Show him how to soar!" And the bird is at it again, entirely oblivious of the fact that he steadily climbs in keys until he goes to pieces again somewhere around G-sharp,

whole octaves higher than the limit of the piano! Such is the character of the singer and his song.

But what a consummate artist he is! Not content with a single key, he deliberately chooses several in major and minor relationship, and elaborates these with perfectly charming arpeggios and wonderful ventriloquous triads, executed with all the technical skill of a master singer.

And what a wealth of melody there is in his varied themes! Note the suggestive motives of the following record:

Wagner himself, in the *Ring of the Nibelung*, has scarcely given a better song to the bird that addresses Siegfried than this which a Hermit Thrush gave me one afternoon on a ferny hill of Campton:

O! wheel-y-will-y-will-y-il.

The little bird sang this strain, together with the Rhine daughter's motive, to Siegfried:

But we have not yet exhausted the resources of the musicianly Thrush. In Richard Strauss's *Symphonia Domestica* occurs this melodic phrase:

Either Dr. Strauss copied the Hermit or the Hermit copied Dr. Strauss (if we choose to think music is sometimes plagiarized), for the bird sang that very phrase, July 1, 1901, in a pasture in Campton, but this way:

It must be remembered, however, that bird songs are most ethereal things, a great deal like the wonderful tinting and delicate spiral weaving in Venetian glass—one must see the color or hear the melody in order to fully appreciate its subtle beauty. The song is charming because of its spirituality of tone and its depth of expression. How can the meager outlines of music notation convey such truths? Who can justly report the Hermit's song? The Hermit's Thrush's tones are silver—burnished silver—and far sweeter than those of any instrument created by the hand of man! There is a sustained tone like that of a flute, then a burst of brilliant scintillating music

> . . . and the song's complete,
> With such a wealth of melody sweet
> As never the organ pipe could blow
> And never musician think or know!

There is unending variety to the uncanny, mirthless performance of two or three Barred Owls, the sounds mostly suggesting demonical and derisive laughter.

Barred Owl

The notes of this Owl are deep-toned and sentimentally expressive of misery—yet that is the human point of view! It's possible that with his *whoo-whoo-whoo, wh-whoo, to-whoo-ah* he's addressing his mate in terms of endearment, but it certainly does not sound that way.

The tones are mostly in E, or not far away from it, close to the middle C of the piano, and they should appear on the musical staff, thus:

The next to last syllable descends the scale indefinitely to *ah* and is entirely different in quality of tone from the *whoos*—it is a sheeplike *blatt.*

Great Horned Owl

The Great Horned Owl is the tiger among birds, destructive to small birds, quail, and even poultry, not to speak of reptiles, insects, small rodents, and even rabbits. From a creature whose habit it is to be out all night hunting, one must expect something gruesome. Certainly this tiger bird cannot be included among the songbirds, but as certainly we cannot throw out his hoot from musical calculation.

The usual syllables of the Great Horned Owl's hoots are

The effect is like that of a bass whistle belonging to a sound steamer heard at a distance, although the tone is not so deep.

*The Great Horned Owl is the only large-sized Owl with conspicuous ear-tufts,
hence his significant name.*

Few writers have given us any record of the scream of the creature:

Fiend!

When that note comes one will think he hears the "crack o' doom." Upon hearing the screech for the first time, one's mind instinctively reverts to those lines in Sir Walter Scott's *Lady of the Lake:*

> At once there rose so wild a yell
> Within that dark and narrow dell,
> As all the fiends, from heaven that fell,
> Had pealed the banner-cry of hell!

The Great Horned Owl's note has the sound of murder in it. No cat on a backyard fence can produce a yell as hideous! So far no one has ventured to call this note the Great Horned Owl's love song.

Screech Owl

The quivering tremolo of the Screech Owl's remarkable voice has in it the very essence of music: the expression of "thoughts too deep for words" embodied in tones of deepest mystery. Whether these tones are properly described as *dulcet* or *bloodcurdling* is altogether a matter of opinion dependent upon the listener's state of mind.

When one considers the character of this Owl's song in connection with his bill of fare, it is not surprising that the former is somewhat indicative of the nature of the latter. What with mice, small birds, snakes, and frogs as a standard diet, why should not one's song savor of the terrible, and cause the listener's blood to run cold! To be sure, that breathless falling of the voice seems to denote exhaustion, and the quavering tones abject terror, but, after all, this is pure imagination, for the next moment the voice suggests that of an operatic singer practicing the descending chromatic scale. Whatever the eerie cry seems like, one thing is certain: all who have ever heard the strange song agree that there is something uncanny about it.

As Simeon Pease Cheney, a naturalist and musician, writes, the Screech Owl "ascends the scale generally not more than one or two degrees" (i.e. one or two tones); "the charm lies in the manner of his descent sometimes by a third, again by a fourth, and still again by a sixth.

I can best describe it as a sliding *tremolo*,—a trickling down, like water over pebbles. Perhaps the descent of the whinny of a horse comes nearest to it of any succession of natural sounds."

On one occasion several summers ago, I was hurriedly invited about sundown by one of the members of the family to investigate a strange voice that issued from the border of the woods near the cottage. Although I knew the note of the Screech Owl perfectly well, this note was less melodic and only remotely resembled it by a curious tremolo:

So I concluded to put the matter to the test by giving sonorously the full Screech Owl song in a series of quavering whistles running down the scale. In less than five seconds there appeared in the dusk of the evening half a dozen young Screech Owls, who flew about with silent wings, and at last perched upon the rustic fence, the arbor, and the old boat which was filled with garden flowers. They had answered my call promptly, and had come to see "what was up!" Their notes were simply weird, a sort of cross between a sneeze and the wheeze of a pair of leathern bellows with the wail of a half-frozen puppy.

W-w-whieu-u-u-u-u-u-u-u! Ah-oo!

Whatever may be our estimate of the Screech Owl's song, the fact remains it is bound up in mystery and carries with it a dubious kind of birdlike despair. This Owl must have accompanied Dante through that dreadful doorway over which was written the fatal words:

ABANDON HOPE ALL YE WHO ENTER HERE.

Shade of Hades! How, oh, how did he ever get back again to sing his woeful song by the light of the moon, in our valleys of peace, and how are we ever to reconcile with reason the statement that this is a wail of woe and a love song into the bargain! That is indeed the mystery of it.

The brilliancy of the Baltimore Oriole's feathers has given him two significant names, Golden Robin and Firebird. The pendent character of his nest has added another, Hangnest.

Baltimore Oriole

The Baltimore Oriole is a sharp-billed, sharp-witted character, and his remarks are as incisive and crisp as the toots of a steam whistle. The following record, which I got in Campton, New Hampshire, will show that plainly:

After the above introduction, these notes were given with the sharp precision of a steam whistle.

The Oriole has a full, rich, round though somewhat metallic whistle, suggestive of the mezzo-soprano, generally reliable in pitch and percussive in effect. However, he is not without the grating, unmusical note that belongs to his family. For sometimes you hear a scolding tone issue from his bill. A bird I heard in the Arnold Arboretum introduced these harsh notes, in a very amusing fashion, in the following song:

The Oriole's only fault is his fragmentary treatment of a good theme, and his chary way of singing it. He is lavish with calls and chatterings, and devotes too much time to preliminaries before he begins the song. The music from a bird in Forest Hills, Massachusetts, is as follows:

It is to be regretted that the bird did not finish, or supplement his theme with the following variation, which strangely enough came from another fellow in another part of the state, Roxbury, a year later:

Occasionally, again, one gets the last half of a tune and never hears
the first part. Here is an instance:

It came from an Oriole one morning in June, as I sat on the piazza of my
cottage in Campton. The bird came and went in a few minutes and I
never got another note from him. But that is usually the way with Orioles, they leave you to find out who has the rest of the tune and where
it will be heard, while they forage among the blooms of the old apple
tree in search of caterpillars.

All of this music is remarkable for its syncopated character. Look at
the bars and it will be seen that the bird occasionally fails to put in an
important note at the proper place, or that he accents a note without
reference to the beat. I have never discovered this character in the song

of any other species than the Oriole. Here is a remarkable instance of syncopation, which I took from an Oriole that sang in the Harvard Botanic Garden in Cambridge, Massachusetts:

The accents are out of all proper relation to the beat. How well the Oriole can deliver a series of thirds in a minor strain the following transcription, however incomplete, will show:

One of the most striking instances of his ability to jump back and forth on an interval of a third is demonstrated in the next song, which I heard early one morning in Springfield, Massachusetts:

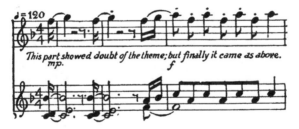

It sounded at first like a boy whistling, who was not quite sure of his theme. But at last I recognized the unmistakably staccato style of the singer—it was the Oriole, and he was practicing a bit of that familiar song in the opera of *Martha!*

> I can wash, sir, I can spin, sir,
> I can sew, and mend, and babies tend.

Common Grackle

There is no discernable music in the Common Grackle's harsh conversational chatterings. His note strongly resembles the noise of a squeaky hinge in an iron gate. If one takes a sheet of notepaper and whistles an octave against its edge, the quality of the tones produced closely imitates the Grackle's best note:

The other queer noises sound like rattling shutters, watchmen's rattles, ungreased cart wheels, vibrating wire springs, broken piano wires, the squeak of a chair moved on a hardwood floor, the chink of broken glass, the scrape of the bow on a fiddle string, and the rest of those discords which commonly play havoc with one's nerves!

The Purple Finch is not purple. I know of no American bird which possesses a single purple feather! What the ornithologist means by purple is crimson.

Purple Finch

The Purple Finch is a warbler with an incomparably sweet warble. There is a ripeness to the voice of the Finch which I attribute entirely to the superior size of his throat and bill. As a consequence, this large bird has a strong and deep voice. He can put much expression in the lower register, and he does so, for his song is sentimental, indeed. Its passionate persuasiveness is truly loverlike and irresistible.

Follow the dots and dashes above with a pencil's point and at the same time whistle quaveringly and rapidly any notes you please, within, say, an interval of a sixth, and you will have an approximate representation of this Finch's song. The dashes represent slurred tones and the dots should be considered as distinct tones given with a musical *shake*. Call this shake a *trill* if you prefer the word, but be sure that you shake or trill on each one of the dots, and do it very rapidly, for the song as above written must not occupy more than three seconds of time! To be more accurate still, it is also necessary for you to burr all the notes, that is, hum and whistle simultaneously. No doubt the directions appear complicated, but how easy it is to follow the notes properly recorded on the musical staff:

This record does not necessarily imply that the bird correctly gave the intervals as they are written—he certainly did not do that. His was a careless, free warble, but it ran smoothly along, up and down, with increasing volume, in exactly the way indicated on the musical staff.

About a year after I took this record, I was greatly pleased to obtain another, which seemed to supplement it perfectly, thus:

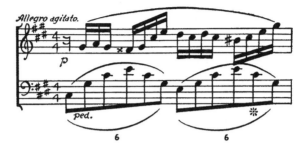

In the examination of these two motives there is every reason to conclude that the rapid and wandering movement that distinguishes both of them demonstrates the real character of the Purple Finch's music. I have never obtained anything more by collecting a score of other songs. All were different, but all followed the same rule: they made first-rate motives for Spanish *tarantelles!* The best proof of that is the comparison of the following song with those which precede it:

And again this rather clever bit with the foregoing:

One is inevitably forced to conclude that the Finch's idea of music is confined to the rapid dance-type in six-eight time to which belongs the *tarantelle*. Perhaps it is proper to prove the case by introducing a bar or two of Chopin's wild *tarantelles* for the sake of comparison:

This may seem a far-fetched simile, but one must not look for similarity of melody between the great composer's work and the song of the bird. It is the musical construction or motive which counts, and who will venture to deny that the bird and the musician worked out their melodies upon precisely the same musical principle?

American Goldfinch

Or if on joyful wing,
Cleaving the sky,
Sun, moon, and stars forgot,
Upward I'll fly.

    —from the hymn "Nearer, My God, to Thee"
    by Sara F. Adams

It would seem as though the writer of those familiar lines must have seen the American Goldfinch's afternoon performance, or she never would have chosen a simile so remarkably suggestive of the joyous heart of the happy little rover. The Goldfinch's habit, particularly in the late afternoon, is to chase about at no great height in the blue summer sky for nothing in particular but the pleasure of the thing, and tell all the world that he is feeling remarkably chipper. As he goes he sings with a thin wiry voice:

Per-chic-o - ree.

He does so rhythmically with his undulating flight, always breaking out with the song just at the crest of the wavelike curve. The swoop downward is, of course, with closed wings, and the recovery is effected at the bottom of the flight by some rapid flips of the wings, then up he goes, and again the cheery notes. One cannot listen to the song of the Goldfinch without laughing involuntarily at the unmistakable glee in which it is executed.

This song, replete with lively humor, consists entirely of a series of rapid chirps. It is impossible to find in this finch's song the melody which is so attractive in the music of the Song Sparrow, or the rhythmic form which makes the White-throated Sparrow's melody so charming. We must look for something else which will reveal the Goldfinch's style, which will be discovered in the following arrangement of dots:

These dots practically mean six or more rising chirps, three or more falling ones, and two clusters of four notes, described by the words *per-*

chic-o-ree. This last he indulges in with exceptional gusto while he is on the wing. The Finch may begin with several chirps in a falling inflection and thus reverse the order given above, and he may also give a different number of chirps, but inevitably at the close of the exuberant chirping he will add his *per-chic-o-ree*, and when he does, he signs his musical autograph as perfectly as he would if he could write at the end of the music bars, "American Goldfinch."

The music on the staff does not appear different from the dots:

The pitch and the key are of no particular importance, but the relative positions of the notes accurately represent the fluctuations of the tones of voice.

There is only one occasion when the Goldfinch has things all his own way so far as forceful singing is concerned. This is at five in the morning, in the maple close by your open window. There he is with fifty of his fellows, and all sing at the top of their lungs whether you wish to sleep or not.

Indigo Bunting

The intensely blue Indigo Bunting, or Indigo Bird, often appears a mere tiny black silhouette against the brilliant sky as he is perched in his favorite commanding position on the topmost twig of a towering tree beside the road, although in the vicinity of my summer home in Campton he is often found, late in the season, hunting for seeds on the roadside. For the best view of his magnificent color we must endeavor to gain a position between him and the sun so its rays will illuminate his intense and lustrous plumage. Excepting his wings and tail which are black margined with blue, his whole body is a deep Prussian blue of an iridescent quality comparable only to that which we see on the Peacock's neck.

The song of the Indigo Bunting is one of the most enlivening little lays. His is the simplest kind of a performance, brief, and at the same time full of beauty and good cheer. But he has no gift of melody, and of sentiment he knows nothing. His is a Canary-like voice, pitched almost beyond the keyboard limit of the piano, and composed of a series of loud, ringing metallic chirp-notes of nearly equal value, which slightly diminish in volume as the song nears the end. Expressed by a group of dashes (these, rather than dots, would seem to be nearer a good representation of far-reaching chirps), the song should appear thus:

$$\text{\textbackslash}/// \text{\textbackslash\textbackslash}// \text{\textbackslash\textbackslash} \cdot \cdot \cdot$$

He always introduces this song with a pianissimo downward chirp, then proceeds loudly with two or three upward chirps, continues with a series which alternates up and down, and finishes with three (sometimes two or four) monotone notes which are remarkably suggestive of the words *fish, fish, fish!* The particular song which is illustrated by the dashes above are again represented by this record:

This is only one of a great number of songs belonging to the Indigo Bunting's repertoire, for no two birds sing exactly alike. There is a striking similarity, though, in the songs of particular families. I have become familiar with the music of individuals belonging to different generations, and the results of my observations when recorded upon paper have proved surprisingly similar. The following three songs belong respectively to a grandfather, son, and grandson. The family resemblance of the music is, to say the least, remarkable:

The third bird sang in 1902 and added one more fish to the song!!

But still more remarkable was the gradual musical development of each song through each season to its complete form. It must be remembered that birds frequently come back to their old nesting places, so when I say that I have noted with interest the musical efforts of a particular individual and his descendants for four, yes, five successive seasons, the records of the findings will not seem so much like results of one's imagination.

Scarlet Tanager

There is a lazy, drowsy, dozy buzz to this beautiful bird's voice which one can only liken to a giant musical bumblebee, or an old-time hurdy-gurdy. The unobtrusive music of the Scarlet Tanager speaks of summer's peace and rest, soft zephyrs blowing over sighing pine trees, and tinkling shallows of woodland brooks.

This most pronounced—and decidedly unique—feature of the Scarlet Tanager's voice is its quality of tone: every note is strongly double-toned or burred. This double-tone can be imitated by strongly humming and whistling at the same time.

The Tanager sings in groups of two, occasionally three, notes. The notes of the Tanager are tied together very closely and are not delivered staccato—all the notes are slurred.

An illustration of the Tanager's song by a series of signs using dashes rather than dots to represent the legato should appear this way:

legato.

— — — — — — — — — — — —

The musical notation of this song very plainly shows the two-note groups:

Observe that all notes are overshadowed by the burr sign. This record was taken from a bird which sang in the Arnold Arboretum, near Boston. Two days later, I heard the same bird sing again, and another little red coat made a charming response in the minor:

I have combined the theme with its response thus:

Possibly there are many who do not esteem the song of the Tanager very highly. To tell the truth, the gorgeousness of the little fellow's costume —a flash of color from the tropics—eclipses his fame as a musician. But we must travel far to hear another voice with such a perfectly delicious reedlike quality, and it would tax the ingenuity of an accomplished whistler to imitate it with any approach to a creditable semblance of its singular beauty.

Cedar Waxwing

The Cedar Waxwing is most certainly a "tailor-made" bird if ever there was one which deserved that significant appellation. His feathers are a close fit, his style refined and irreproachable, his orderly appearance is in sharp contrast with that characteristically disheveled morsel of bird-life which we call the Chickadee, and his dignified carriage is an unexceptionable model for other members of the feathered tribe. His colors—and conduct as well—are quite almost to the point of being Quakerish: upper parts a soft tone of light brown graded to gray on wings and tail; head conspicuously crested; region about the eye and beneath the bill black.

The handsome Cedar Waxwing is a bird of beauty, but alas for his song! It does not exist, or if it ever did it is now reduced to the level of a pianissimo imitation of the whistle belonging to the peanut roaster which sings on the corners of city streets.

I have managed, not without some difficulty, to locate the note of the average Waxwing at E-flat, just three tones beyond the limit of the piano!

Ornithologist and naturalist Bradford Torrey writes pleasingly about the almost unbroken silence of this bird's life, and adds: "Of course I refer to the Waxwing whose faint, sibilant whisper can scarcely be thought to contradict the foregoing description. By what strange freak he has lapsed into this ghostly habit, nobody knows. I make no account of the insinuation that he gave up music because it hindered his success in cherry-stealing. He likes cherries it is true, . . . but he would need to work hard to steal more than does that indefatigable songster, the Robin."

Their quiet unobtrusiveness, their silence, their gentle manners and refined appearance, always make the Cedar Waxwings peculiarly attractive to the bird-lover, in spite of the fact that they have an unfortunate reputation for being overfond of cherries. Cherry-stealing is the chief complaint against this bird.

Red-eyed Vireo

The Red-eyed Vireo is omnipresent, persistently loquacious, indefatigable, and irrepressible! He has something to say at all times and under all circumstances. He is a restless fellow and is seldom in one place for more than a few seconds at a time. He is in every orchard, along every highway and byway, and on the margin of every wooded hill throughout the country.

He is easily recognized by his intermittent song. All through the long summer day he sings his rhythmically broken, interrupted song. The dots show the disconnected character of the song perfectly:

The musical notation in general appearance is not unlike that of the Robin:

But there really are great differences. The Red-eyed Vireo's voice is pitched on a higher key, the notes are more rapid although the pauses are much longer, and the whistle is an apparently clear one by no means running along in unaltering three-note groups.

The mechanical rhythm of the Vireo's song is perfectly expressed by a series of rapid beats or taps or notes. There are two, three, four, or even five notes in a group, and these are given with such rapidity and with such lack of true pitch that one ought not to expect any semblance of tunefulness. The bird cannot sing a connected song; his attempt is a sort of musical hash, a potpourri of tones, not melodies.

However, not the best songster in the country on the morning of the rarest day in June can give us a livelier, cheerier roundelay. In the gayest of spirits the Red-eyed Vireo sings from early May until the middle of August, and if some hot day in midsummer you enter the woods, and far up among the treetops where the light is greened by the forest's multitude of leaves hear the following song,

you may be sure it's that of the Red-eyed Vireo. The notes are clearly whistled and are pitched very high, there is scarcely a suggestion of the overtone, and the groups themselves are closely connected—in fact, slurred.

Henry Ward Beecher, crediting the Vireo with a devotional nature, has said of him, "He pauses between each morsel of food to give thanks to Heaven," which is exactly the case if one considers the half-note rests as the time required to devour morsels! But Wilson Flagg's description of the song places the bird among the clergy, and one wonders whether the Vireo is not after all a religious character, for he says, "The Preacher is more generally known by his note, because he is incessant in his song. . . . Though constantly talking, he takes the part of a deliberate orator who explains his subject in a few words and then makes a pause for his hearers to reflect upon it . . . 'You see it— you know it— do you hear me?—do you believe it?' " If we imagine that the bird is expressing his exuberant feelings by idle chatter as he searches for his breakfast and thinks his wife ought to be by his side to share it, I should venture to suggest he said this: "Fat worms . . . plenty to eat . . . Gobble-em up . . . they're sweet. . . . Come dear . . . don't delay . . . Fly this way . . . I'm here!"

Warbling Vireo

The best way to find the Warbling Vireo is to be on the lookout for a group of agitated, wagging leaves. There, in the midst of the disturbance, a tiny, restless, busy figure will presently appear and disappear before one can adjust the opera glass—it is he! Throughout May and June he makes his home among the maples and elms of Plymouth, New Hampshire, and Cambridge, as well as suburban New York. His time is spent among the treetops exploring every leaf and twig with tireless energy.

Watch him closely if opportunity affords, and you will find his music and business are inseparable; he is a busybody, occupying every moment, never stopping to sing, never idle. His refrain is: "Can't you see it's best to sing and work like me!"

The Warbling Vireo's attempt at music does not resemble a song as much as it does a bit of a fantasia, caprice, or the somewhat rapid movement of a sonata. His song is a continuous warble exclusively his own. His voice is a rambling soprano. In construction his tune is a smooth, continuous flow of about nine or more notes of equal value. There is no other Vireo that sings this way.

When the bird begins, he runs on until his song has finished, without break, pause, or any unevenness whatsoever. Here is a record from Saxton's River, Vermont, taken May 23, 1901:

There is little variation in the character of the Warbling Vireo's song. Sufficient proof of this is found in a record I made in Cambridge, Linnean Street, two years earlier—May 21, 1899:

This song is constructively identical with the record taken in Vermont.

One needs to bear several points in mind in learning the character of the Warbling Vireo's music. It is almost entirely without definite pitch —that is, the bird does not seem to sing in any particular key. Furthermore, the notes are closely connected together and seem to be rolled around in his bill like a sugarplum, but in spite of this effect they are delivered staccato. The last note in particular is struck abruptly, as though it were red-hot! Finally, it is evident that a slight overtone distinguishes every note. Each note gathers force as it goes, and the last note will be found to be the highest in the great majority of songs.

Although note for note the fifth measure of Chopin's wild but beautiful *Fantasie-Impromptu* does not correspond with this Vireo's song, it cannot be denied that there is a striking similarity in the construction of the two fragments:

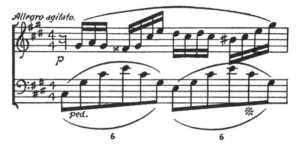

Both bits of music roll triumphantly toward a high note in a sort of spontaneous ebullition of feeling, and there the matter ends—with the Vireo. But Chopin goes on, and his sprightly embroidery of tones is ultimately succeeded by the more substantial form of a slow and dignified melody. If we take the Vireo's song and give it the advantage of a harmonious setting, the result is not a bad one:

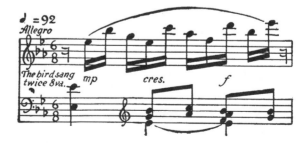

Yellow-throated Vireo

My first acquaintance with the Yellow-throated Vireo dates back many years to the day my Manx cat entered the studio with the little creature in his mouth quite dead. This less common Vireo is beautifully marked—the back is a clear olive modified to gray on the rump with two white wing-bars, and the throat, breast, and a ring around the eye are bright yellow. I had been puzzled by the distinctly different character of two songs I had heard, evidently belonging to two species of Vireo. These proved to be the songs of the Red-eye and the Yellow-throat.

There are certain radically opposite characteristics to the songs of the two species. It is commonly said that the Red-eye has a soprano, and the Yellow-throat a contralto voice. That is a fairly good comparison as the

Red-eye really does pitch his voice in a high key and the Yellow-throat in a much lower one. But the most striking difference between the voices of the birds is less a matter of key than quality of tone — in a word, the Yellow-throat's notes are completely dominated by overtones, and the Red-eye's notes are not. To imitate this effect, I hum any tone down in the base and at the same time whistle up high in a very slurring fashion the three or four notes common to the Yellow-throat's song. Of course, music of that nature does not bear any relation to the full, pure tones of a contralto singer. It is nearer the truth to say that the Yellow-throat has a violin quality to his voice, or better, a reedlike quality.

For the rest I may add that the Yellow-throat's tempo is much slower, and that he does not indulge in such an interminable bout of singing!

The Red-eye takes life much less seriously. The deliberate way in which the Yellow-throat sings separates his song from that of all his relatives. He is never in a hurry, and after singing three or four clusters of slurred notes, thus,

he gives you plenty of time to think the matter over before he makes another remark. At the time of the Boer War I imagined this bird was telling me all about it:

Certainly one finds the word *Buluwayo* fits a particular group of notes remarkably well.

There is no variation from this kind of singing so far as I am aware, except that the little fellow occasionally talks to himself sotto voce, as many other birds do, and his remarks become musically incoherent. I recollect whistling to a Yellow-throated Vireo one day, in his own fashion, when we met in the Botanic Garden in Cambridge, and to my infinite surprise he dropped his stereotyped song and ran rippling along among a lot of trills and warbles, *pianissimo et gracioso!* That was a surprise, and I wondered whether it was meant to be a tender love ditty, with myself mistaken for the charming Juliet! Perhaps so, who can tell?

Nashville Warbler

This delightful little Warbler with a jolly song and engaging, cheerful manner is relatively common throughout New York and New England. Its favorite haunts are the half-overgrown pasture, or open woodland where the trees are mostly very young. I recollect spending an early morning in May on a hilly pasture watching no less than fifteen Nashville Warblers joyously chasing each other about among the tops of the young spruces and firs, and singing incessantly.

The song of the Nashville is a delightfully typical one with little or no rhythmic variation; it skips along in a most lively fashion and ends with a ripple! Expressed by dots, it should appear thus:

♦　·　♦　·　♦　·　♦　♦　♦　♦

Or, if one prefers syllables, thus:

te-dum', te-dum', te-dum', te-dum', te-did-dle-te-dee!

Here is my notation of the song previously expressed in the series of dots:

There are a few varieties to this form—like this one where the trilled notes are low instead of high, thus:

And still another where the bird doubled up on the two first rapid trill notes:

In every case the Nashville accents—or makes "lame-legged"—one or the other of his slurred notes, and that ought to be a very strong point in the identification of the song.

I remember hearing my friend, Professor J. B. Sharland, tell his quartet to sing the notes in the opening bars of Rossini's *Carnovale*, as they were written, "lame-legged," thus:

The rhythm is exactly that of the Nashville's song!

The Yellow Warbler's nest is built of fine grasses, plant fiber, and fern down, often lined with horse hairs.

Yellow Warbler

This is one of our commonest Warblers, and it is often, but most mistakenly, called a Wild Canary. The prevailing color of this species is yellow throughout, bright on the crown, greenish on the back, and brownish on the tail. An interesting character as well as a beautiful one, he is quick in his motions, even more rapid in song, charming in his almost fearless manners, and marvelous in his sagacity.

One of the most interesting instances of bird-nesting I have ever known was that of a Yellow Warbler who had chosen an upper branch of a Scotch rosebush for her dwelling. She had arranged the nest in such a position that eventually a large cluster of the yellow roses bloomed directly over her head, thus effectively shielding her from observation.

The voice of this Warbler is loud and exceedingly penetrating. Traveling in an express train over the Boston and Albany Railroad, I have more than once clearly distinguished the song as it slipped in through the ventilators of the car, and really dominated the din of the train.

There are several types of the Yellow Warbler's song, two of which are extremely common. Here is one:

• • • •   • • ＼

The notes are all of equal value, the interval is approximately a third between the fourth and the fifth notes, and the seventh (the last note) slides downward—by a slur apparently another third. The bird sings in presto time, and his tones are clearly and loudly lisped at the very top of the keyboard and perhaps three notes higher. Here is the musical notation:

The second common type can be demonstrated this way:

There are three downward chirps of an interval approximating a fifth, then the single higher note (the half of the chirp) followed by two notes just a third lower, then a last highest, thus:

The songs which end with the high note are many. Here is one,

and here is another, showing how the type remains the same though the bird rings a change in the positions of the last few notes:

These last two records were taken in Cambridge and the Arnold Arboretum between May 14 and 21, 1901, after I thought I had gauged all the possibilities of variation in the song of this species! Eventually I have had to add still another type to my collection, which strangely reverses the order of the song, thus:

Others have recorded several forms of the song different from mine. It is to be hoped future observations will not reveal new forms, otherwise, one will be inclined to charge the Yellow Warbler with musical plagiarism! But from whom could he steal such forms? Certainly they do not accurately represent those of any other Warbler, and who can find fault with a bird who chooses to strike out experimentally on new lines!

Black-throated Blue Warbler

The Black-throated Blue sings a characteristic but not soul-inspiring song. His is an effort without a tune, a sound comparable to an accidental scraping of the bow over the cello strings with the musical tone somewhat decimated.

The song is generally described in syllables, thus: *zwee-zwee-zwee-e*. John Burroughs says it goes with an "upward slide and the peculiar *z-ing* of summer insects, but not destitute of a certain plaintive cadence." It is one of the most languid, unhurried sounds in all the woods. I feel like reclining upon the dry leaves at once.

The Black-throated Blue's song is short and deliberate, and the extremely high tone is dominated by a correspondingly low drone—the buzz which Mr. Burroughs likens to the *z-ing* of an insect. I can imitate it by simultaneously humming and whistling through the teeth. The range of voice evidently consists of a fifth interval, and commonly a

fourth. There are three, four, and sometimes five ascending notes to the song, but these are so closely run together — i.e., slurred — that their individuality is lost. By lines the song should appear thus:

In musical notation it should appear thus:

He is essentially a woodland bird, but the fearless and curious little fellow frequently visits the roadside and the vicinity of dwellings. On one occasion I had the pleasure of seeing him hop to within three inches of my shoe in a persistent endeavor to find out whether I was myself a bird or held one captive. Of course, I was conversing with him in his own language, but I have not an idea what we talked about!

Black-throated Green Warbler

It was a brilliant day in early June in the foothills of the Franconia Mountains: the clouds lay piled away up in the north over the blue and jagged horizon line formed by Lafayette, the Notch, and Cannon Mountain; below, in the broad sunlit valley, the beautiful Pemigewasset wound its silvery way between the wooded hills; the little hill on which I stood was carpeted with the rich rusty-brown pine needles of past seasons, and here and there a gray lichen-covered boulder cropped out from among the green ferns and the forest's russet floor. It was indeed a lovely spot. Some bright-faced, appreciative girl would have said, had she been present, "What a sweet place for a picnic!" Perhaps I thought so, too, for, at the moment, I heard, among the green, swaying, sighing pine branches overhead, a tiny bird sing:

It was the song of the Black-throated Green Warbler. This bird is not in such a hurry as the others of his family, and his song is distinguished for its suggestive rhythm and its deliberate tempo. Of the usual five notes which he sings, the two next to the last are burred and the others are clear:

If you whistle this song between the teeth, and burr the two notes next to the last by humming and whistling simultaneously, you will obtain a very tolerable idea of the Black-throated Green's song. The song must be whistled in the high register or one will not get a proper impression of it.

I find the Black-throated Green is not at all particular about syllables. For, on May 6, 1902, at ten o'clock in the morning, I heard him singing amid the thick branches of a Norway spruce on the grounds of the Harvard Astronomical Observatory in Cambridge, this next sarcastic refrain in more syllables than the law allowed!

Sweeping skies with a spy-glass!

Here is another song from Arlington Heights, Massachusetts,

which is likened to a bar of the familiar old sea-song "Larboard Watch" in which the notes are dotted, which is the only difference:

Lar-board watch a-hoy!

Ovenbird

Here is the case of a David with the voice of a Goliath! This is the noisiest Warbler in the whole family. Listen attentively, and if you hear a wild, lawless kind of a song, do not doubt for a moment that it is the Ovenbird. The time, most likely, will be late afternoon, just when the other birds are beginning to sing vespers!

The Ovenbird's song has the effect of the Bobolink's spontaneous outburst, but it has neither the force nor the tinkling glass quality of that bird's song. The Ovenbird's song is really remarkable for its spontaneity and exuberance, but beyond that I do not think it can be called extraordinary, as it carries no suggestion of melody.

The Ovenbird's syllables have been excellently represented by Mr. Burroughs as

teacher, *teacher*, TEACHER, TEACHER, *TEACHER*.

Naturally we would accent that word on the first syllable, but I insist that on the contrary the bird lays particular stress on the second syllable, thus: *tea-CHER*. Musically considered, that accent on the second syllable is of greatest importance, for it enables me to express with accuracy the character of the Ovenbird's peculiarly noisy song with musical notation:

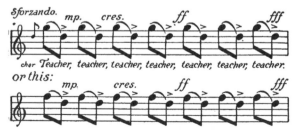

The tone of voice is a bit unique; it is dominated by no overtone, yet it is not a clear whistle. It sounds, in fact, as if the bird threw it out from his cheeks rather than his lungs. I suppose most musicians would call it a "mouthy" tone notwithstanding its fortissimo character! The woods fairly ring with the sound, and the voices of the other birds, for the time, are completely lost.

Song Sparrow

This is the bird that sings best of all—sings under all conditions of weather, at all times of day (and sometimes at night), in every month of the year, and with the cleverest understanding of melody.

I had grown quite familiar with a bit of melody coming from a bird nesting near a boat landing on the river, which ran thus:

But before long there came a day when the sun refused to shine, and the clouds hung dull and gray over the river meadow. I was at work on the piazza next to my studio listening, as usual, to the sparrows, when a pathetic strain caught my ear; it was the same familiar melody, but strangely enough rendered in the minor key. What did that mean? Was it the same bird or another? I dropped my paintbrush, seized my opera glass, and ran to investigate. Yet, there was the bird in his customary position on the top twig of the bush next to the one in which his mate had built a nest. (He wisely refrained from singing in the same bush which contained the nest, for that might lead to discovery.) I looked for the nest and it was there, too, but there was no mate. "Aha!" I said to myself, "a case of domestic infelicity." So, when the little fellow sang again the doleful strain, I fitted, in imagination, these words to it:

Wail, wail, fickle wife is she, Flown away and left me!

Then, taking my cue from another singer, I whistled a reply as follows

Sad, sad, what a tale of sorrow! She may return tomorrow.

and went back to my neglected paintbrush. Sure enough, on the following day, which dawned bright and clear, up from the meadow came the happier strain in the major key, with the welcome news

True, true, very true you see, She's come again to live with me.

so I knew everything was all right down there. Nonsense, all this, everyone will say! But what about that melody in both the major and minor keys! That remains a remarkable fact. The Song Sparrow has the ability to render a motive in both the major and minor keys, just exactly as Verdi has done in the ninth and eleventh bars of the "Di Provenza" (be sure to read them).

The Song Sparrow is also one of the very few birds who is able to sing half a dozen songs, each of which is constructively different from the other. The Thrushes are far more gifted musicians, but they lack the versatility of the Song Sparrow.

Presumably everyone knows his call note—a metallic chirp—but through sheer multiplicity of motive, I suspect his song is not always as distinguishable. Especially as it often develops a distinctly local character. For instance, the Song Sparrows of Nantucket apparently sing with higher-pitched voices, more overtones, and less regard for the usual accented opening notes than do those of the White Mountain region. The birds about New York, on the other hand, accent the first few notes and then often ripple along in canary-like trills. But the fundamental character of the music is never changed; it is apparent in a series of accented, sustained tones (generally three) at the beginning, the middle, or the end of the song. But usually at the beginning there is a rapid succession of about six notes—or better, a tone interrupted a number of times, a group of tones separated by well-preserved intervals, and the contrastive coloring here and there of distinct overtone. It is evident, therefore, that the mechanical rhythm of this bird's song is no strong factor in its identification; it is too variable to be depended upon. One song is likely to be in two-four and another in three-four time, and the listener is compelled, rather, to listen to those striking mannerisms of the singer, which will nonetheless surely reveal his identity.

Now the style of the Song Sparrow is unmistakably evident: he devotes himself to pure, simple melody, and is in consequence the best example of the song motive among all the members of the feathered tribe. The Oriole may sometimes equal, but he can never excel him in this respect; moreover, the Oriole lacks versatility. Here is the song of one bird:

There is a swing and an accent to these notes which perfectly express an exultant feeling, something akin to that so eloquently given in the first bars of Siegumund's love song in the *Nibelungen Lied:*

To be sure I enlarge the musical significance of the Sparrow's song by setting it to a piano accompaniment, but I question whether it is possible to recognize the value of the melody without the setting. Notice how much expression is dependent upon those accented first notes, and how the mannerism distinguishes the singer, for nearly every Song Sparrow seems to stand by the rule!

Another little bird gave me a fragment of a Chopin-like mazurka. The motive was suggestive of something more, which I never got. It ran thus:

Rup-it 'rup-it rup-it, spits wig a gee!
N.B. Do not mind the syllables, they are not more nonsensical than those employed by the ornithologist for tunes!!

and that was very aggravating, for it should have been rounded off thus:

But it never was rounded off, so I had to accept the fact that even the Song Sparrow does not always know how to finish a thing.

There is a very good story told of Beethoven which illustrates in an amusing way the annoyance of a "tie-up" in music. The good old master had gone to bed and was tossing restlessly on his pillow because his nephew, Carl, downstairs, was repeatedly practicing what a musician would call a harmony in suspension; something which goes like this:

After a while poor Beethoven, who could not stand that sort of thing indefinitely, shouted down to his pupil, "Carl, give us the resolution."

But Carl misunderstood the command, thought he was told to stop, and went to bed leaving the tones "hung up." That was beyond endurance, so Beethoven arose, hurried into his dressing gown, ran down to the piano, struck a modulation or two, and landed fortissimo on the proper key thus:

That settled it; he could now go to bed and sleep peacefully!

This suspension or incompletion of a musical idea is what we are always regretfully discovering in a bird's song, and the attempt to find a finish anywhere usually results in failure unless we piece two tunes together. The little songster's conception of music is limited to the abstract. What should he know about a finish? His song is an overflow of good spirits, and you must chop off his head if you seek a finale. His song is simply a bit of untrammeled self-expression that goes on like Tennyson's brook, notwithstanding human rules about "resolutions" and "finales."

But the Song Sparrow is not always unsatisfying in the matter of a conclusion, for here is a double record obtained from a little fellow who knew how to supplement a really beautiful theme with another similar one, which brought it to a most satisfactory end:

I am disposed to believe that everyone who will study the music of the Song Sparrow long enough will inevitably come to the conclusion that he is Nature's cleverest song genius. Indeed, in justification of such belief, I have only to call attention again to the extraordinary melodic value of the songs above recorded and say to the one still unconvinced, "Match these if you can!"

Vesper Sparrow

The Vesper Sparrow is a splendid singer chiefly for the reason that he seems to consider song a serious piece of business which must not be interrupted by any of the other duties of life. He will never be found feeding and singing at the same time. When the Vesper Sparrow sings he selects a high perch (in Campton his favorite place is the ridgepole of the bowling alley which belongs to the hotel near my cottage), and begins a season of song which is likely to last without interruption for nearly half an hour!

Words are entirely inadequate to express a musical idea, but if I had to demonstrate the nature of the Vesper's song that way, I should supplement the words by lines, and say the structural part of it resembled the gable end of a roof, thus:

$$\wedge$$

The first half ascending in four or five clearly whistled notes, and the last half descending in about as many high-pitched, rapid, Canary-like

The Vesper Sparrow is very fond of dust baths. In fact, he neither bathes in nor drinks water at all, getting all necessary liquid from his diet.

chirps or trills. Now, suppose we resort to a series of dots to represent the song's form:

The principle of the gable-roof lines is still maintained, and if one de-sires to hear the rhythm thus represented, it can be obtained by tapping each dot carefully with a pencil.

The music of the song properly written on the staff resembles the nursery melody of "Lord Bateman."

The bird's rendering appears as follows:

I consider this one of the best and most characteristic productions of the Vesper, though his confreres in other parts of the country by no means cling close to its melodic form. Naturally, the birds of every

locality develop certain provincialisms in song, and the Vesper is no ex-
ception to that rule. But he certainly does not attempt to depart from
the rhythm which characterizes the song of his species. For example, the
previous record came from a bird more than a hundred miles away from
another in Vermont which sang the following:

This record shows that the ascending and descending divisions (or
halves) remain in the same relative position, although they are in a
measure doubled, while the sustained tones begin and the chirped or
trilled tones end the song precisely as they do in the first record.

The character of the trills, or chirps, too, needs some explanation. In
the first place, such notes cannot be properly called *trills*. I only employ
that term in the popular sense of its meaning rapidly repeated notes.
They are slurred tones covering intervals of indeterminate length rendered in a shrill register beyond the limit of the piano keyboard, and,
so far as the ear is able to detect, a whole octave higher than the sustained tones which form the first half of the song. This trill is far from
unusual among the Finch family. I call to mind a Canary, a splendidly

trained singer, who could render an operatic melody in clear whistled tones, moderately high, and at its finish strike at once into his natural wild song, which must have been considerably over an octave higher. That bird was owned by a barber whose shop was near Union Square, in New York City, and its value was some fabulously high figure which I do not remember.

The Vesper Sparrow sings with both style and feeling. He always begins pianissimo, swells in a fine crescendo, and diminishes as he descends to a tone very near the tonic:

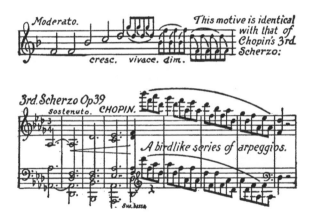

He sings from sunrise to sunset with a sweetness and joy at once inspiring and beautiful. He is not unsociable, for it is his habit to remain in the road hopping or flying just ahead of you at a safe distance, showing the white feather as his tail spreads in flight if you get too near.

White-throated Sparrow
(Peabody-bird)

The song of the Peabody-bird is remarkable for its rhythm and its pure, clear-whistled tones. Anyone who can whistle can imitate it. I have never yet failed to call the Peabody-bird from a considerable distance by imitating his song. In more than one instance it has been possible by this means to draw a dozen or more birds about me, all of whom were devoured with curiosity to find out why such a great hulking, wingless bird should be familiar with their own language.

There is considerable variety in the Peabody-bird's song. It begins with long tones of equal length; then three clusters of three short tones, each cluster being equal to one of the long tones. How plainly a series of dots illustrates this:

◆　◆　◆　◆◆◆　◆◆◆　◆◆◆

and how equally plain the rhythm appears on the musical staff:

This song embraces an interval of a fifth. Here is another which includes one of only a major third:

And here is yet another confined to a fourth:

This is one of the commonest forms of melody which is employed by all composers. It occurs in the opening bar of the love song sung by Turiddu before the curtain rises in *Cavalleria Rusticana*:

The similarity of this air to that which the Peabody-bird sings is at once apparent.

Another song with the interval of a fourth, which a bird gave me in the White Mountains, is strongly reminiscent of the "Di Provenza" from Verdi's *La Traviata*. This is what the bird sang:

And these are the first bars of the simple but beautiful melody from the opera:

Certainly the resemblance between the two songs is striking.

Occasionally the Peabody-bird attempts a high pitch which he is unable to sustain, and then we hear him drop down the scale by easy steps like a musical sigh, thus:

The tone here expresses as much discouragement as the words which accompany it. There is a sort of "Heigh-ho, fiddle-de-dee!" character to the music which makes one think the little bird looks upon life and its cares as a tough problem! It's not unlike the sentiments expressed by Carmen when she appears in the first act of the opera and sings that love is a willful wild bird with whom it is dangerous to have any dealings, and advises her admirers to let him alone. The music expresses all the discouragement which is embodied in the Peabody-bird's song; observe how the notes drop down the chromatic scale in precisely the same way:

The little Peabody-bird sings Carmen's song in Tuckerman's Ravine under the shadow of Mt. Washington, Turiddu's song under the brow of Mt. Tecumseh, and the "Di Provenza" from *La Traviata*, in the Pemigewasset Valley. The question arises, what will he do next, somewhere else?

White-crowned Sparrow

The White-crown sings leisurely in a tree by the roadside and waits for an answer:

♩ = 88
Moderato. *cres..* *f* *dim*

My song is ever of thee

In another moment there comes a response from a neighboring tree, and White-crown number two continues the love song:

Then number three supplements the two foregoing songs by a marked variation:

And again a fourth bird rounds off the tune:

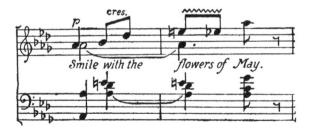

But the birds are not content to let well enough alone, and still another fellow puts in his song to prevent anything which might seem like a finale:

For human musicians may come and go with all their fine theories and cadences and cadenzas—what does the little bird know of these? His one idea is melody—unrestricted melody such as he is accustomed to hearing in the songs of his associates. Probably he does not suspect that these have been handed down to them through a long line of ancestors, and that he will, in turn, hand down what he has learned to the generations of the future. Why, therefore, should a finale have any place in the bird's song?

Field Sparrow

The Field Sparrow is certainly Nature's best exponent of the principle of plainsong, i.e., the chant. One need not for a moment suppose it is necessary to have a wide range of voice and sing a catching tune to creditably produce a song. No, music is the artistic expression of thought and character, and for that reason the pathetic monotones of the Field Sparrow charm us. We do not care whether he sings a tune or note; he may keep straight along on one note or not as he chooses. We are satisfied to know that he sings with a depth of expression unsurpassed by any of Nature's greatest songsters.

My best opportunity of hearing many Field Sparrows singing together has always been on the rugged ground of the Middlesex Fells, near Boston. (A Field Sparrow may frequent an old worn-out field, but the cultivated one is not his choice. He likes a spot more or less overgrown with weeds and bushes.)

Anyone with a knowledge of Western music would unquestionably pronounce the song of this species one of the best melodic demonstrations of a combined accelerando and crescendo. The little musician has explored the whole realm of sound, and condensed its beauties in perfection into one short song:

The whistles are all on the same pitch and only the middle tones rise or fall, as the case may be, progressing to a final so-called trill. This song is confined to the narrow compass of a minor third, and the tones ascend. In another song, the little singer reverses the order and descends the scale:

In still another, he proceeds on the diatonic instead of the chromatic scale, thus:

and reminds us of the opening notes of the chorus in *Martha:*

Nor is this all the Field Sparrow can do. He frequently gives us a perfect example of what the music teacher would call acciaccatura, a succession of short grace notes, thus:

There is a certain reverential character to the Field Sparrow's song, too. When the shadows lengthen into irregular blotches of misty lilac on the slopes of the stony pasture and the light has turned golden in the west, somewhere in the tangle of blackberry briers not far away there is a modest singer filling the silent air with the sober monotones of a vesper hymn. It is the Field Sparrow, and possibly he is singing—who shall say that it is not?

> Softly now the light of day
> Fades upon my sight away.

Yellow-breasted Chat

The Chat is an eccentric character: shy, retiring, it chooses the dense thicket for its home. Certain strange and sudden monosyllables of the Chat sound exactly like *Quirp! Chuck! Cop! Chack! Charr!* It is risky to place these on the staff lest one should think they are really musical tones. They are simply indescribable noises, that is all.

In the line of music, he can, however, give us an excellent ritardando and diminuendo, a time arrangement exactly the reverse of that of the Field Sparrow:

But one cannot call such a series of clucks obviously musical. This performance is a combination of voice tones without either key or pitch.

I might add that the bird frequently gives a number of clear whistles of accurate pitch; but these, though I place them on the staff, prove to be such fragmentary bits of the song that it would be useless to depend upon them for purposes of identification:

The fact is that the Chat may be considered a mere chatterer.

Catbird

The Catbird has an uneasy and restless disposition, shifting his perch, dodging between the leaves, bobbing his tail up and down, raising his crest, puffing out his feathers, and otherwise showing his disapprobation of the intrusion on his private grounds whenever you approach to watch him. His only note at such a time is the harsh and nasal *meow* so suggestive of the cat.

There is a certain lawless freedom to the song of the Catbird, for he does not entertain any regard for set rhythm, and he proceeds with a series of miscellaneous, interrupted sentences which bear no relationship with one another. His music set on paper in a thoroughly complete manner would appear thus:

It is like some long rigmarole, which is humorously incomprehensible, though the bird apparently considers his remarkable strophes both serious and important. Listen to him sometime while he is singing in the shadowy tangles of the briers and willows through which winds the brook with gurgling, petulant impatience, and you will hear some unmistakable tuneful expostulations, persuasions, and remonstrances. When he has finished you will wonder what it was all about—whether he was telling the brook that such fretful slipping over the pebbly shallows was an undignified and needlessly noisy proceeding!

The Catbird's music is all his own, but he suggests the songs of various birds—some of the notes are like those of the Robin, others resemble

those of the Red-eyed Vireo, and still others those of the Chat. His voice is not as strong as that of the Thrasher, nor can he sing as well as that bird, but his song is refined, sprightly, and interesting although disjointed, jumbled, and lacking in melody. The fact is, he is an imitator. He can imitate anything from a squeaking cartwheel to the song of a Thrush. He intersperses his melodic phrases with quotations from the highest authorities—Thrush, Song Sparrow, Wren, Oriole, and Whippoor-will. The yowl of the cat is thrown in anywhere, the gutteral remarks of the frog are repeated without the slightest deference to good taste or appropriateness, and the harsh squawk of the old hen, or the chirp of the lost chicken, is always added in some malapropos manner. All is grist which comes to the Catbird's musical mill, and all is ground out according to the bird's own way of thinking.

Meadowlark

An unquestionably pathetic, if not mournful, song rises from our meadows in spring and early summer which may be attributed to the Meadowlark. This bird is one whose slurred whistle conveys an impression quite the opposite of cheerfulness. The strain is a dolorous one and the most optimistic interpreter could never clear it of a certain plaintive quality.

That is wholly due to the bird's habit of slurring his notes. It would be impossible to represent these notes by dots—only a series of curves can describe his indecisive attempts at hitting a tone:

If you whistle the three curves above—providing there *is* such a thing as a curving whistle—you will get the Meadowlark's song. In other words, a tone must be given descending or sliding to the first tone below, then repeated with a slide to the fourth tone below, and then repeated the third time exactly as it was given at first.

But that is, of course, one song, and we must remember if fifty of the birds sing there will be fifty songs! And in every one of them the principle of the slur is absolutely maintained.

In the summer of 1903 I heard in Nantucket a bird which sang with charming accuracy the following first two bars from Alfredo's song in *La Traviata:*

But this was sung in the same pathetic way in which Violetta sings it a little later in the same act, when she finds she must give up Alfredo. There is an unmistakable pathos in the bird's song.

It is not always the case, however, that the music is pathetic. One afternoon, while crossing the downs of Nantucket, I heard a bit which was decidedly reminiscent of the song and dance with castanets in which Carmen attempts, in the opera of her name, to lure José away from his duty:

This, it must be admitted, was not sung in quite the lively way the libretto would demand, but the melody was correct:

A moment later, however, another bird spoiled the whole effect by finishing the song the wrong way, thus:

Meadowlarks, and birds in general, for that matter, are prone to take unwarranted liberties with operatic scores.

A Meadowlark in the vicinity of Boston offered the following bit from Gilbert and Sullivan's *Ruddygore:*

He hailed the bridegroom but drew the line at the bride. Why did he not finish?

I am unable to say whether he had a grudge against the bride or simply forgot his part!

Of all birds, the Meadowlark is the most provincial. He does not migrate very far from his breeding place, or perhaps does not migrate at all. As a consequence, his character is perfectly reflected in his song that, too, is strikingly provincial. The birds of Vermont sang a song so strange to me that at first I did not recognize it. Again, the birds of Nantucket sang a different song. And now, after a disinterested consideration of the whole matter, I have come to consider the song of the birds in New Jersey one of many forms, each of which is distinguished by some local characteristic. In every case there is *one* thing we can rely upon as unchanging, and that is the descending slur.

Ruby-crowned Kinglet

As a rule, the Ruby-crowned Kinglet is so absorbingly interested in the business he has at hand that he sometimes allows one to approach—if one is quiet and cautious—within ten feet of him, and thus observe his sprightly and restless movements. The bird is often found among the spruces which clothe the slopes of the White Mountains.

The Ruby-crown commonly trills first and sustains a few notes afterward. Notice this point in the following songs obtained in Smuggler's Notch, under Mt. Mansfield in Vermont:

The song was both wonderfully limpid and smooth-flowing though interrupted by the Wren-like grating notes which really deserve no place on the musical scale. The trills or reiterations upon the triad show the unique character of the song.

(There was merely the impression of the G minor key)

The song of the Ruby-crowned Kinglet is astonishingly loud and clear for so tiny a singer, and it is praised by all who are acquainted with it for a most remarkable sweetness and brilliance of tone.

American Robin

After an extended acquaintance with the songs of a number of Robins one finds that they are all distinctly different, and that one specimen in about ten is, musically speaking, worth all the others put together!

The Robin varies both in song and in quality of voice, but every individual singer adheres closely to a common mechanical rhythm. The notes are generally delivered in groups of three; sometimes a sprinkling

of two-note groups occurs, but this forms no considerable part of the song. Expressed by dots the song would appear thus:

••• ••• ••• •• ••• ••• •• •• •••

The form is that of a disconnected warble in rather a narrow compass of voice, and with very slight variation.

Some birds sing with an excellent pitch, others ramble along with no particular regard for key or melody. The following is an excellent example of good melody for a Robin; notice that the fellow has made his own response to his own motive, a thing which not every bird can do by any means:

The key was a perfectly obvious one and the song though sung in the usual wild, disconnected way of the Robin was excellent in its intervals and its note values.

How characteristic it is of the Robin to sing in a nervous, hurried way, without ever a thought of the value of a sustained tone such as that which the Hermit Thrush gives us. When something or somebody disturbs the Robin, to resent the interruption he offers an emphatic remonstrance in the diatonic scale or something akin to it, thus (I wish this did not remind one so much of the opening notes of that popular piece, which is doomed to an ephemeral existence, called *Hiawatha*):

How natural it is, too, for another fellow to enter the breach and without altering the key revise the arrangement of the theme, extend it, and proceed on independent lines in more insistent tones very nearly as follows:

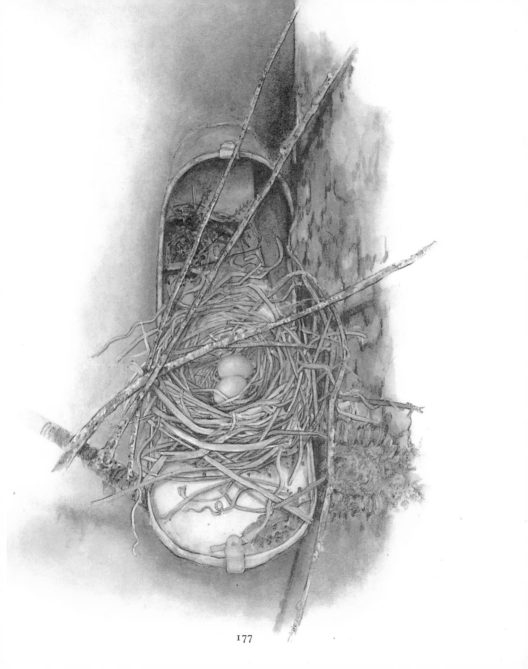

And if you listen to the first fellow, how out of patience he seems to be with the turn matters have taken! This is the way he seems to scold in an indignant fortissimo voice:

After that we are perhaps favored with a duet; but the singers stick to their own ideas and melodies regardless of each other, and the music becomes an unintelligible jumble. There is certainly a bit of rivalry going on, for Robin number one is getting excited and is hitting wildly at his notes in *allegro agitato* time in good earnest!

Another interruption occurs and one of the birds fairly yells to the other in high staccato tones:

Although he is a noisy fellow, there is a host of good cheer in the Robin's music which the discriminating writer in A Masque of Poets early discovered:

> In the sunshine and the rain
> I hear the robin in the lane
>   Singing "Cheerily,
>   Cheer up, cheer up;
>   Cheerily, Cheerily, Cheer up."

These words fit the following music fairly well:

Bluebird

While the air still has a piercing chill and the cold gray clouds chase each other across a forbidding sky, the keynote of the spring symphony is struck by a little Bluebird who is perched somewhere among the bare, brown branches of the old maple beside the road, or the apple tree in the orchard:

You may call that the Bluebird's note if you choose, but there is a certain unsteady, bouncing character to it which can only be properly expressed by the grace note and the succeeding three notes:

It is precisely the Bluebird's method to handle all his notes that way; the little singer does not seem to know how to rest steadily on one tone! There is a pleading quality to his voice—a plaintive tenderness which is entirely due to the unsteady character of his notes. No Robin sings this way, however similar the notations of the two birds appear to the eye. For, if one expressed the Bluebird's music by dots it would look exactly like that of the Robin, and as a matter or course musical notation is little more than the scientific placing of such dots. It is therefore necessary to pay strict attention to the Italian directions for expression, as these

This is one of the earliest birds to arrive in the spring. It is a question which we are likely to meet first, the Bluebird or the Robin, but not infrequently a flash of the cerulean color tells us the Bluebird has won the race.

will show the fundamental difference between the songs of the two birds.

There is so little variety in the music of the Bluebird that the following record suffices to represent its fixed character. The scope of the voice is limited to a fifth, but as a rule the bird sticks pretty close to a minor third, and to a minor key:

Even when a number of Bluebirds are singing together very early in the morning (when one would suppose a song would be at its best) I have scarcely ever heard a singer suggest the major.

Here is a song, the minor key of which was unmistakably evident, that came to my ears at half past five on a morning in June, 1902, in Dublin, New Hampshire:

The tones are unmistakable, quavering, tentative, uncertain, a bit tender and sentimental, and far more appealing than the robust ones of the Robin.

In Conclusion

It may be quite difficult to think that a bird should have actually sung one of the melodies recorded in this volume. If so, the best way to overcome the difficulty is to take ears as well as eyes into the fields and listen not to every singer at once but to one at a time. Perhaps, then, after the unraveling of Nature's tangled gold and silver threads of melody, one strain may be heard far more beautiful than any of the musical fragments recorded here. The little bird is Nature's exponent of the joy of living; his song never dies with him: he passes it on.